Beyond Being Good

Ovations for Beyond Being Good

Katrina's words are like those of a sweet friend, sharing her stories and struggles while inviting you to dig deep into how God is unfolding a perfect, beautiful story in your own life- no matter how broken it may feel. I love Katrina's perspective and encouragement to lean into your faith - to take hold of God's outstretched hands wholeheartedly and without abandon. Beyond Being Good was a joy to read and is sure to encourage and inspire women everywhere.

-Emily Ley, Author of A Simplified Life, Creative Director of The Simplified Planner

Every "good girl" needs to read this book! Katrina challenges her readers to move from pretense to substance in their relationship with Christ. Her honesty and transparency encourages us to let our hair down and be real with God. Katrina's words are convicting, yet inspiring; her thoughts richly metaphoric, yet down-to-earth. It is packed with so many pearls of wisdom, that I consider the entire book a gem! Beyond Being Good is destined to catalyze a generation who is more than nominally Christian, one who boldly lives out their identity in Christ!

-Isis Smalls, Empowerment Speaker, Bestselling Author of *Beauty in the Making*,

Katrina writes, 'When you're loved well, you live well.' These words of truth bring hope to everyone on a quest to live life to its fullest. The author illuminates hope to broken spirits and healing to wounded hearts. To learn we can truly live with integrity, character, and Christ's redeeming love make this a must-read! I highly recommend this addition to your personal library.

-Dr. Susie Shellenberger, Speaker, Author and Creator of Brio Magazine

As the standards of morality shift all around us, Katrina repositions the Gospel as the true test of goodness. Beyond Being Good is going to unleash the next generation of female Christ followers to move past a shallow desire for approval to a passion filled calling to serve Jesus. Her words and her genuine heart are evident and I am so thrilled for each reader who dares to turn these pages.

-Kat Armstrong, Speaker, Writer, Founder of Polished Ministries

Katrina's heart for people is evident in every page of this book. A relevant massage for this generation and the ones to come; she explores her past to show how she fought through the "being good" trap and into being profoundly present and whole. This book takes you on a journey of self-reflection, ultimately ending in the loving embrace of our Heavenly Father. Katrina opens her readers up to be authentic in their vulnerability by simply saying, "I'll go first"!

-Amanda Roman Leak, co-author of
The One: An Amazing Love Story Starts with You

I'm grateful to know that I'm not alone in this pursuit of being more than just a "good girl". I believe this book has offered us all a challenge to increase, not only in staying far away from the lies of "Checklist Christianity", but most importantly that we truly dive into the depth of our personal intimacy with the Lord. This book encourages the reader to fully receive and trust God's love so that when the day comes, we can be His ready bride! All I have to say is, 'consider the challenge accepted.'"

-Trinity Anderson, Singer, Song Writer,
Vocalist for William McDowell Music

When I read a book, I desire to feel connected to the author and a sense that each word I'm reading is backed with substance beyond mere opinion. Katrina writes in a way that is powerfully vulnerable, amusing and rooted in God's word. Her use of scripture and personal stories intertwine her message in a refreshingly authentic way and I can truly say I closed this book with a better sense of who I want to be as a woman and as a Christian! Beyond Being

Good is a celebration of the transformation that God desires to create in each of us, no matter where we may find ourselves in our current situations.

-Hannah Leigh Walsh, Missionary and Founder of Symbols of Grace

Katrina's message expands our sometimes 2-dimensional thinking, as Christian women. We get so caught up in the doing for others, personal successes, and personal pride in ourselves, that we forget it's all about a RELATIONSHIP with the Father, not just an acquaintance with Him. This book comes at the right time for women who are seeking more in their relationship with Christ than just doing the right things and being good.

-Jasmine Powers, Worship Leader for 8th Day Church, Co-Founder of Studio Powers Dance Studio

Katrina's words truly ministered to me in several situations and I have no doubt that others will discover healing through her vulnerability and transparency. Her use of scripture and personal stories tug at familiar places and points directly to our loving Savior! This book is sure to be a blessing to those in need of healing from the deception of perfection and for others who will keep it as a reminder of the commitment they made to God and to themselves. So sweet. So sincere. So genuine!

-Andrea Coleman, Technical Account Manager for Microsoft and Women's small group leader

Beyond Being Good

Seeking Christ's Perfection for Our Imperfect Hearts

Katrina McCain

Elm Hill

A Division of
HarperCollins Christian Publishing

www.elmhillbooks.com

Beyond Being Good
Seeking Christ's Perfection for Our Imperfect Hearts

Published in Nashville, Tennessee, by Elm Hill, an imprint of Thomas Nelson. Elm Hill and Thomas Nelson are registered trademarks of HarperCollins Christian Publishing, Inc.

Elm Hill titles may be purchased in bulk for educational, business, fund-raising, or sales promotional use. For information, please e-mail SpecialMarkets@ ThomasNelson.com.

Library of Congress Cataloging-in-Publication Data

Library of Congress Control Number: 2018931637

ISBN 978-1-595557599
ISBN 978-1-595546913 (eBook)

To Jarrett and Kailyn, who continue to love me as I am.
To my family, who raised me to know and love Christ.
To my Pearls, who show me every day
that living for the Lord is possible.
And to my little one, who is still growing inside me.

For I am confident of this very thing, that He who began a good work in you will perfect it until the day of Christ Jesus.

~ *Philippians 1:6*

Contents

A Note from Katrina

Dear friends,

It is my absolute joy to share these next few pages with you. Odds are, you are in a place where you are ready for the Lord to increase His presence in your life. Maybe you've been living for Jesus for a long time, or maybe you have a new curiosity for Christ; either way, it's an exciting place to be in!

Let me first be upfront and say that I am the last person qualified to write a book like this, because I am not always good; though I wish I were. I have struggled my entire life with mistakes, accidents, bad choices, failures and temptation. I'm not perfect and I never will be. I know you aren't, either. So, instead of reading this book from the angle that you will be learning how to overcome and be better and live more successfully, I want you to turn each page knowing that I, the writer of this book, have been where you've been. I am just like you: a woman who desires to live the life that God has called her to; a woman who knows there is more to life than what she can earn or pay for; a woman who senses deep within her heart that she was created for greater and for more meaningful and abundant living; a woman who knows she is nothing on her own without Jesus.

Beyond Being Good is my gift to the dozens of women who have come to a place in their lives where they are ready to surrender their hearts and their efforts to God. It is my hope that, from the scriptures, stories and encouragement provided in this book, every reader will begin to operate in a more authentic understanding that Jesus loves you exactly for who and where you are.

My desire will always be to spend my life pouring into other women and encouraging them—letting them know that it's not always going to be perfect, and it's not always going to be pretty or predictable, but you can live for Jesus in an impactful and beautiful way! Beyond Being Good is an extension of this message and the mission I feel God has called me to. This book is for all of you! May you glorify God, even in the messes, and may you know, once and for all, that His love for you has nothing to do with your performance or your ability to be a "good girl".

In Christ's Love,
Katrina

PART ONE

WORKS IN PROGRESS

CHAPTER 1

Dingy Dresses

In the midst of a most beautiful wedding ceremony, you find yourself among joyful family and friends. As the usher escorts you past each pew, you notice that the church is filled to capacity. He motions for you to take a seat, right up front. The décor is impeccable, and the ambiance is breathtaking! All the guests show up in their best, exchanging admirations and congratulations for such a special day. You are honored to have been invited; and you, like everyone else, stand at the music's call for the bride to enter. As most people do, you steal a quick look at the groom who is front and center, waiting to receive his bride. He looks proud and handsome and confident. "I bet he's going to cry when she walks in," you think to yourself.

With a rush of wind, the doors open, and the bride stumbles into the chapel, laughing obnoxiously over her own clumsiness. Stumbling down the aisle in a dingy dress, she is tattered and dirty from the hem up. Her hair is disheveled and undone; her lipstick is smeared and chipped fingernails dangle from her hands. It is clear to you that literally, she must have just rolled out of bed.

"She looks a hot mess," you hear someone behind you whisper. Sad to say, but true, you agree. She finally makes it to the altar and reluctantly takes the hand of her groom. On what should be her most perfect day, she complains during her nuptials and winks at other men as her betrothed lovingly and sincerely expresses his love for her. She begins to yawn in front of all of her guests, impatiently waiting for the ceremony to come to a close. She admires her ring and watches it gleam in the light, but she's unconcerned with her groom. She pulls out her cell phone and begins to scroll while saying a quick, "I love you, too." It's not a pretty picture, is it? Odds are, you might even feel uncomfortable at the thought of even attending a wedding like this. Maybe, if you were one of the guests, you'd have serious concerns, not for the bride, but the groom.

Regardless of this bride's seeming lack of love and sincerity, her groom continues with his vows, to your dismay. He patiently waits for his bride to participate with her whole heart. He stays committed and expresses his love for the whole world to see, in spite of how slack she is in her disregard towards him.

"Unbelievable," you think to yourself. From the corner of your eye, you notice some guests getting up to leave. It's clear that they came to see something real. They thought they would be witnesses to the real deal—a true ceremony of love, but instead, all they see is someone unprepared and insincere. She is merely going through the motions. Inside, you are dying from such a spectacle. You are uncomfortable, and you want to leave, too. How could anyone go through all the trouble of announcing an engagement and preparing for a wedding with such a questionable attitude? Don't judge too hastily. Imagine yourself as that sort of bride.

We are all imperfect. We all have tattered hearts and ragged places from mistakes made in fleeting moments or circumstances we wish we could have avoided. Yet these realities don't disqualify us from God's perfect love. He longs to mend what's been broken, beaten and bruised, and He asks us to allow His goodness to heal us, instead of us trying and striving to cover up the truths of who we are and what we are dealing with. Our redemption requires more than good deeds or personal improvements. Our wholeness is dependent on God's love and His goodness. But are we truly living our lives believing this truth?

I have concerns about young women in my generation—those who claim the name of Christ, yet are not actively preparing themselves to be united with Him in glory. Like this bride, there are so many Christians in our culture who live out of excuses handed to them by the world and take advantage of the spiritual gift of grace. We've become comfortable in our brokenness, but that is not the abundant life Christ desires to give us. Each of us, in some way or another, have conformed to the world's standards, trading the eternal goodness of Christ for a version of our own, and therefore sacrificing the power of God in our daily living. A dying world is looking at the habitual compromise of Christians with uncertain agony. They see the scriptures we post on our social media pages, but then they notice we are still promoting promiscuity in the way we dress and in the way we date. They see we are still bashing our husbands or excusing bad habits. With hands lifted high, we profess Christ with our lips, but not our hearts. The world sees our hypocrisy and onlookers are confused and painstakingly uncomfortable with the display of "Christianity" that some of us portray. They came to see a wedding with true love and real hope and genuine faith in Christ. They came to see restoration, and forgiveness and the beauty of grace through Jesus. But sometimes, I wonder, what do they really see? I'm concerned that some of us don't even realize we look a hot mess!

But God's goodness changes everything! It's His life and His light that restores our hearts to reflect His own. Yes, we each hope to be "good women," "good daughters," "good wives," and just plain "good people", but is that really all we're living for? Is that all that we are striving after in the midst of cultural conflict and uncertain times? As Christian women, what is our purpose? Is it just to go to church? Is it merely to try and fit in some Bible reading time a few days a week? Is it only to do good things and say kind words? The truth be told; you don't have to be a Christian to do those things! In fact, there are many different faiths that teach similar "Christian" values. There are unspoken social rules that praise you for doing what is kind and fair and condemn you for anything less. Even good-natured atheists make an effort of performing good routines in their own lives without the salvation of Jesus or the influence of the Holy Spirit.

So, when you think about it, doing good things is not the epitome of the Christian's purpose. Our good deeds do not give us more validity before God than the deeds of those who are not Christians, and our temptations and brokenness are not fouls that disqualify us from our faith. We have been called to live above the positives and negatives that seek to distract us from our true purpose. Our real identity is never based on our efforts to be good. We consider ourselves "good girls," but our own goodness does not result in holiness. Only the presence of Jesus can bring this. Only His purity and perfection can change our hearts.

I gave my life to Christ as a child, but it wasn't until I was twenty-four that I came into a true relationship with Jesus. Throughout high school and college, I claimed His name but did not reflect His heart. I did not represent Him well. I know I am not alone. Many of us are guilty of having claimed to know a God with whom we didn't truly have a relationship with; perhaps the relationship wasn't much because we just didn't know any better or because we were trying to live by rules in our own strength. Regardless of the reason, who we say we are living for and how we live must line up. Jesus is coming back! He promised us He would come for us in John Chapter 14. But are we living out our lives in preparation for THE BIG DAY? Are our earthly relationships marked by the fruit of the Spirit? Are our thoughts aligned with the promises of God? Sadly, if we are honest, the answer might be "no." Sadly, if we are honest, some of us are living our lives in dingy dresses.

Like you, there are many lessons that the Lord is teaching me. Some of them I have to keep learning over and over again as I grow in God's grace. None of us are perfect, after all. But in our learning, let's never overlook the importance of representing Christ well. Each of us is a bride! Even if you are not married, each day of your life is preparation for a wedding with the Lord. And our daily choices, attitudes, and conversation should serve as an invitation to those around us that they ought to be preparing themselves for this wedding, as well. When we name the name of Christ, there should be more to it than mere Christian platitudes or churchy lingo; it should be real! The lives we live should be filled with the hope and faith that Jesus is the answer for all of our hearts' needs. Loving Jesus and sharing His love is not about our own goodness; it's about His, and it is our calling to live this out with sincerity and grace from the Holy Spirit.

As women of the Lord, we are called to be a sweet-smelling fragrance wherever we go.

2 Corinthians 2:14-16 says, *"But thanks be to God! For through*

what Christ has done, he has triumphed over us so that now wherever we go he uses us to tell others about the Lord and to spread the Gospel like a sweet perfume. As far as God is concerned there is a sweet, wholesome fragrance in our lives. It is the fragrance of Christ within us, an aroma to both the saved and the unsaved all around us. To those who are not being saved, we seem a fearful smell of death and doom, while to those who know Christ we are a life-giving perfume" (TLB).

Our lives are not offensive, but sweet. Will we offend? Sometimes. But the offense should be caused by the conviction brought on by the Holy Spirit who uses our sincere love and obedience to Christ as a way to prick the hearts of those who do not yet believe.

Living out a prosperous walk in Christ means a change in our entire existence such that we begin to operate in the fullness of our calling and the freedom of God's love. This walk comes not because our attempts at "goodness" impress Christ, but because He is intensely in love with us and invites us to experience His goodness in every area of life. As we sojourn through these pages together, my desire is that we will begin to take a look at where we are in Christ and devote our time and attention to praying over where we would like to be. At no time should we find ourselves satisfied as if we've made it. Our heart's desire should always be, "Give me more of Jesus!" But we don't have to be fanatical or get all weird about this. God invites us to be who we are because He made us, and He alone truly knows us. But we do need to come to the understanding that being a spotless bride is not something we can accomplish outside of Christ. We can't attain that status on our own. We do not have what it takes to be pleasing and perfect in the eyes of God. On our own, we are not good. As the Bible states in Romans 3:10 "*No one is good—no one in all the world is innocent* " (TLB). And I'm sure we all have past personal stories to prove it! We are truly broken people, yet a ferociously loving God dearly loves each of us. We are valued, called, and given purpose, in Jesus' name. Know that these truths can only be ignited and fulfilled once we enter into a relationship with a Savior who gives us all of His goodness in exchange for our dinginess.

Questions for Discussion

1. What were your thoughts about the example of the bride with the dingy dress? In what ways did the literal and spiritual implications reflect on your relationship with Christ?

2. In your walk with Christ, what lessons are you learning? How are these lessons shaping your natural and spiritual life?

3. Have you ever experienced the pressure of trying to be a "good girl?" In what ways has the label of "good girl" hindered you from a living a life of grace in Christ?

CHAPTER 2

Neon Lights

My parents taught me about patience and waiting on the Lord. They taught me scripture and how to pray for God's will, but in my haste to be important, I resisted what I knew from them and exchanged it for what I wanted. And what I wanted was to be seen.

Neon lights always seem intriguing from afar, as do the lures of lust and social acceptance. This allure for acceptance deceived me in ways I never expected. Deeds done in secret feel fun for a while. Life was all cool and exciting, and I felt I belonged for a time. But the problem with neon lights is that they don't illuminate very much. Shadows slip in under the dim glow, and though you can see, there is no vision. The neon lights of this world beckon our attention, but they are so deceptive. Many of us have fallen into the trap of being persuaded by the glow and enticed by the shadows that assure secret pleasures and empty promises of no regrets. But when the true light shines, and night turns into day, our deeds done in shadows shame us and we cower deeper into hiding.

"We 're not bad people," we tell ourselves. "We've done nothing worse than anyone else." So we glance around trying to find someone guiltier than we are, and we clench to the checklists we measure ourselves by, like security blankets. We seek proof that we are still "good girls." We compare ourselves to others to tear them down and lift ourselves up. We believe the lies that good intentions are enough for righteousness. Though our standards shake underneath our hypocrisy, we insist we will do better and get ourselves together. We have all been there. We have all been victims of bad choices, shaky excuses, regrets, guilt and shame. We have all spent time in the dark. Maybe some of us are still there.

To be honest, my time in the dark was terrifying, because I knew the truth. I am a pastor's daughter, after all. My sweet parents instilled scripture and Biblical knowledge in me as I grew up. I attended a primary private school and was allotted a Biblical education. I knew all about Jesus and the cross, God, and the devil. I knew the facts, but I didn't receive them as applicable truths in my life for a time. Upon entering college, I chose to live in unbelief. Although I would have said I was a Christian, my choices proved otherwise. The thoughts I harbored and the attitude I flaunted were all contrary to the love of Christ. Deep down, I knew I wasn't pleasing God, but I didn't have a hunger to change. So I sat in back pews and allowed my mind to wonder in other directions. I'd flip through the pages of scripture without real understanding of what I read. On the surface, I was the picture of perfection compared to others in the college culture. I was innocent of certain social sins—you know the ones: sex, drugs, and drunkenness; I avoided these like the plague. Virginity was my trophy, and I paraded it around, as if it made me perfect—it didn't. It's a pure heart that God is after, and mine was far from it. I was guilty and ashamed, but unsure of how to be truly free. I made good grades. I had pretty friends. I drove a decent car, and I wore nice clothes. I draped myself with external façades of righteousness, and my pretense was so comfortable, no one needed to know I was a fake—a real hypocrite. In church, I raised my hands, and I sang choruses in soprano of words I'd memorized but did not live out. People admired me for my abstinence, and I served my volunteer roles with smiles. But, I was most unsatisfied, even with my "good girl" label. The masks I wore appeared beautiful, but it was all a lie.

Sooner or later, life has a way of exposing unstable foundations. As the truth emerged from underneath my pretenses, everything began to collide for me. I could no longer handle all that I knew I should be and all I was trying to be. My hypocrisy brought me to my knees at a point in my life where I was losing all hope. At the peak of my loneliness and the climax of my brokenness, God saved me. And I will never fully grasp why.

Vain Pursuits

It's taken the entire decade of my twenties to accept God's love for me. The last decade of my life has truly molded me to acknowledge that there is a loving God who has more for me than I thought I wanted for myself. I now seek Him beyond my wish list and have learned how to encounter Him in the living of each day. I invite Him into the content of every decision and the internal motives of my heart. It took my darkest moment for God to shine His brightest light, and drive all of my shadows away.

There was definitely a long span of time when I wanted nothing to do with the life that I now live. I was running in the opposite direction, trying to stay afloat by what I presumed a "good girl" was supposed to be. To the beholder, I was as innocent as they come, but my heart was weighed down with selfish ambition. I suffered silently as I attempted to ease my conscience of a life apart from the experience of a relationship with God. Makeup didn't cover up the impurities that I tried to excuse away. Fashion didn't free me from my secret struggles. Vanity and vain pursuits were my closest companions, but they took from me more than I wanted to give. The Bible tells us that, *"Charm is deceitful and beauty is vain, but a woman who fears the Lord shall be praised"* (Proverbs 31:30 NASB). I learned this scripture in the fifth grade, but I had no idea what it meant. Throughout college, I looked for ways to get praise and tried to create a sense of beauty through my own goodness. All these efforts left me in great need.

Looking back, I can see how much God loved me. I can see that I was His treasure—the one He pursued. Though my life was crumbling as a result of the absence of God's holy presence, He saw something worthwhile in me. He saw a lonely girl with her identity eradicated—a soul lost and unaware of her own value and purpose. I was His little lamb who had wandered off and gotten caught in the thicket of life. He saw me when I was doing bad things—things of which no one else was aware. His eyes were on me when my heart collapsed from the weight of regrets as I failed at being good. He viewed me in my vanity and still called me beautiful, not for how I looked, but for who I simply was. He loved me.

In the darkest times of my past, this loving God illuminated my heart and offered me forgiveness. He freely extended His salvation to me, and I desperately snatched it from His hands, knuckles pressed together with a measure of faith and a hope that each promise He offered would be real. He is offering you the same.

Each day since, my journey with Jesus has been one of steady progress. He's taken me further than I ever dared to dream. He's given me a purpose that He continues to unveil, and He's offered hope and love and beauty in place of my imperfections. He's adorned me with grace and with high expectations for the future of my life here on earth as well as the hope of the glory of His kingdom yet to come. It's not been an easy journey; I must admit this upfront. I have fallen more times than I have run, and I've confessed shortcomings more than I've proclaimed victories. I have sacrificed more than I'd ever anticipated; but the glory of the reward of His presence and favor has made it worth every challenge that's been set before me. This life in Christ is not easy, as it calls for absolute surrender. And there are no guarantees of a trouble-free existence. Even when we walk with God, challenges will come. Yet, Jesus promises, *"My yoke is easy."* In Matthew 11:28-29, He says, *"Come to Me, all of you who weary and have heavy loads. I will give you rest. Follow My teachings and learn from Me. I am gentle and humble in heart. You will have rest for your souls"* (NLT).

Life is hard, but God is good! His love gives us rest for our tired souls. He is the source of our goodness, and His love is our victory! He takes each step with us and carries us in our failings. To anyone who would dare tell you that life with Jesus makes everything perfect with no more problems, it isn't true. Even in Christ, there are still mountains to climb and storms through which to navigate, but we are never alone. We have the help of the Holy Spirit. We have the Comforter. This life with Christ will involve going through the storm and the fire from time to time, but our joy is that we will not be overtaken. Jesus makes this life beautiful. Nothing else will ever satisfy apart from Him.

Loved

Though I am still growing, I am finally learning what a relationship with Jesus really means. It's not about proving yourself or cleaning yourself up. It's not about portraying a beautiful and perfect life. Being a Christian goes beyond self-effort to eliminate our imperfections or attempts to live a sinless life. It's about allowing Christ to indwell our hearts and live through us. Jesus already lived the sinless life for us. All we need to do is receive His love and believe His words are true. When you are loved well, you live well. God loves us beyond the capacity of anyone or anything this world has to offer. Realizing that our lives were meant for His love gives us the perspective we need to live in the abundance for which we were created. We were not born to merely survive. Our lives have promise and a destiny; and Jesus' love, expressed through His word, unlocks those callings within our hearts. Living can be complicated when we live outside of our purpose, but there is freedom when we embrace that we were born to be loved by a great God who desires a relationship with each of us. Our self-righteous attempts to be good will never suffice. We are not meant to live apart from abiding in Christ. His invitation is always open, and His heart is always calling us to Himself. John 15:5, 9-10 states, *"For apart from Me you can do nothing....As the Father has loved Me, I also have loved you; abide in My love. If you keep my commandments, you will abide in my love"* (BSB). Answering that call to abide in Christ's love requires trust and obedience to scripture, which takes courage and faith. Loving God means pleasing God, and that response is dependent upon accepting that He loves us unconditionally. He calls us daughters and friends. His love is deep and sweet and so very freeing! And no matter how much we try, we can never earn the beauty of His great love. *"We love Him because He first loved us"*, 1 John 4:19 tells us (KJV).

Part of my problem from my past is that I compromised and abandoned so much of my heart for the sake of feeling loved and accepted by my peers. I lost so much of who I was. But in Christ we gain, we don't lose. His gift of life is free and available for the asking. He doesn't charge or trade. He gives all that He is for all that we are! I've never known a love like His, and it grows stronger within me every day. He gives me all that I need to be successful, including friends who can walk alongside me and encourage me as I keep my eyes stayed on Him. Everything I tried to earn on my own, He has given me freely out of His abundance and out of His pleasure over me. The "good girl" identity has no place in the kingdom of God, and laying down the burden of that title has set me free emotionally and spiritually. I don't have to be what people expect. I don't have to keep a checklist of what I have and haven't done. I'm not obligated to present myself in order to impress others. In Christ, I have the freedom of being who He is shaping me to be. He is the Potter, and I am the clay (Isaiah 64:8). My soul is being refined, and I'm in no rush to get through this journey. The love of Christ is perfecting and transforming me on a daily basis, but not for temporary social approval. With each new day, I live to receive God's love—a love that is unconditional from the start.

I am no longer lonely anymore. I am no longer a drifting wanderer or a fake. The girl I used to be is consistently being replaced with the girl I should have been all along. Through this process of living with Christ, I am gaining understanding of who God is and how very much involved He wants to be in my life. The Lord desires to do the same for you. You have great purpose and a beautiful future in Christ! You are not a mistake. You are not a disappointment. You have done bad things. So have I. You have been a liar. So have I. You have chased neon lights. So have I. Yet we are still invited to experience the fullness of living in the true light of the Lord! Neon lights eventually go out. They burn out and then get thrown away. But the glory of the Lord is eternal, and His light will shine forever.

Temptation

For twenty-eight years, I remained a virgin until I was married. Yes!!! It is possible!!! You can do it in Jesus name!!! But being a virgin didn't make me more loved or less loved by God. Virginity was not my guarantee for God's approval. Believing I was "OK" before God because I practiced celibacy was a huge mistake on my part. My attempts to be good only opened the door to other temptations and personal failings. In our culture, goodness, like beauty, is in the eye of the beholder. The world says what is good for one person doesn't mean the same is good for someone else. And what was great yesterday is not guaranteed to be good today. We are presented with temptation when our own goodness becomes our standard and the measure by which we say we are accepted by God. But according to scripture, we are to shun self-righteousness, which is the act of creating our own goodness apart from God (Romans 10:3). When we focus on our own sense of "goodness," we operate under a deception, which distracts us from our need for salvation. God totally bases His acceptance of us on our acceptance of Christ's shed blood on the cross. His blood paid for our sin. When we focus on who we are, what we are doing, and where we are trying to go, we get lost every time. It's like looking at your own feet, instead of following the navigation system. When we take our eyes off of Jesus, we can't expect to stay in God's light. Eventually, we will wander off and find ourselves in situations and circumstances that we were never intended to experience. Our sense of direction is broken. Proverbs 16:25 says "*There is a way that appears to be right, but in the end it leads to death*" (NIV). We cannot rely on our own "goodness," because it doesn't exist. Psalms 14:3 makes this clear: "*But no, all have strayed away; all are rotten with sin. Not one is good, not one!*" The perfection we seek is not self-made; it's created in Christ (TLB).

As we continue through this book together, I want you to know upfront that I love you and I'm praying for you. We each have different stories, but we can all relate to being without Jesus at one time or another. Maybe you are in a place where you are still trying to figure out if you even need the Lord. I hope this time we share together will unveil many truths about God's love and how it can change you forever. It's all about Jesus! There is no remedy within yourself that will make you a "good girl"; there is only a good God and He loves you. And bless the Lord, He loves me, too! I know I don't deserve the goodness that He's offered me. However, my life today is full of hope and promise, and my identity is based in the truth. Jesus has given me freedom and clarity of mind to live above the culture. I devour a divine grace that transcends merely existing and takes me into truly living. I'm writing this book to encourage you that you are not alone. If you are still searching, I've been there, and I understand. If you are still struggling, well I've been there, too. We may have had different struggles and different experiences, but underneath it all, we are the same. We are so-called "good girls" who are desperately and divinely loved by a good God!

Questions for Discussion

1. "Realizing that our lives were meant for God's love gives us the perspective we need to live in the abundance for which we were created." What does this mean to you?

2. When did you realize that your goodness was not the standard that God desired? How has this realization affected your life and your relationship with Christ?

3. "When we focus on our own sense of "goodness," we operate under a deception, which distracts us from our need for salvation". Ponder this statement. What is the deception and what is the remedy for it?

CHAPTER 3

Bathroom Prayers

I was wearing a mini skirt when I first heard from the Lord. I was twenty-two and on my way to a college party. It was the biggest party of the semester, and so it was expected that anyone who was someone would be there. I had endured some pretty major life-altering circumstances, including the untimely death of my college boyfriend. Devastation doesn't even adequately express the feelings of agony I felt following his murder. The grief was indescribable and my despair devoured me. Being young and immature, I turned to social media as an outlet—a medium to express and release my thoughts and emotions. I'd write him letters and post them to his page, pouring my heart out for a sense of relief and release of my pain. As a result, I found myself to be the topic of dorm-room gossip, as various classmates and so-called friends privately dissected my situation amongst themselves. I was embarrassed and desperate and I felt so alone. I had hidden the entire relationship from my parents, and I felt uneasy about going to them for counsel. People told me I would get over my loss, but as months went by, the sorrow got worse. Eventually, I decided that I needed some help.

For seven weeks, I snuck into the Campus Counseling Center at UNC Charlotte, with my jacket hood pulled over my head—I didn't want anyone to see me there. I didn't want the stigma that comes along with seeking professional counsel. I wasn't crazy. I was hurting and I longed for relief and peace from very haunting thoughts and troubling fears. I was in deep mourning and agony. I tried to pray, but felt too guilty to do so. I felt his death was my fault. I felt my rebellion and my disobedience resulted in this punishment and I felt isolated from God and from myself. In so many cases, it takes the brokenness of our very soul to bring us to the Lord, because, well, who else can mend a soul but Him? When you don't think you need God, you don't reach for Him. But at some point, in spite of our friends, our successes, our outward beauty and seeming stability, life has a way of bringing us down. In those moments, only the Lord can lift us up. At twenty-two, I was way down. I had some major problems, but I was still trying to fix things on my own.

That night, as I was preparing for the party, my bangs hung heavily down my face, and I began to stare at my reflection. My nails were painted, and my skin was glowing; my makeup was the final touch. Though I looked good from the outside, my heart was on the ground. Most of my friendships were crumbling all around me. I felt misunderstood and alone, yet I found comfort in my sweet friend, Samantha. I was humbled by her compassion for me. During this time in our lives, so many changes were driving us in different directions. My self-absorption prevented me from being the friend that she needed; still God used her to love me at my lowest point. In spite of my selfishness, she stood by my side when no one else did. She understood my heart, even when I was incapable of understanding hers. That's the problem with selfishness: it blinds you to what really matters. So many people and opportunities went overlooked by the blindness I endured due to my narcissism. It was this spiritual blindness that prevented me from seeing Christ, as well.

After 3 years of partying, I became exhausted by the routine of the club scene. I loathed the stench of party boys and their alcohol. Though I refused to drink, that stance didn't stop people from annoying me with offers. I went through the motions of typical college girl behavior, but it disgusted me. The idea of being grabbed for a dance by sweaty strangers and the mundane ritual of giving out my number, only to encounter yet another disappointing potential relationship, repulsed me; but that was the college life I had cultivated. I really wasn't confident enough to live any other way or to do anything different. I was desperately trying to be someone I wasn't. At the time, I was beginning to make good money as a model and wasn't sure what to do with my earnings. I saved a little bit but spent most of it. Foolish. I wanted to be happy, and it seemed like those who had the most fun were those who felt free to do whatever they wanted. I wanted to do what they did and look like they looked and talk like they talked. They seemed so free, and I wanted to be free like them. But all my attempts to find freedom only bound me the more. I couldn't understand why. What was I not getting? What was I missing?

In the core of my heart, I knew I was wrong. Bible stories and church sermons echoed in the back of my mind, so I turned my trap music...umm...rap music up louder! My sweet parents tried so hard to advise me and guide me, but their "Jesus" bothered me. I couldn't understand why they wanted to stifle my life. I couldn't understand why they didn't realize that I was doing fine—my good grades and virginity were still intact! I read my Bible devotionals sometimes, and I attended my mom's Care and Share women's groups, when I could. My life wasn't perfect, but I was managing. I was in magazines for crying out loud! I was on TV and only two semesters away from graduating with a real college degree! I didn't need their help; I just needed their support. I felt judged by their advice as I was too lost to know the difference between being judged and being loved. The enemy of my soul had definitely succeeded in blinding me.

Trying to blend in during college was arduous. It required both compromise and disobedience. Eventually my kid brother started making similar choices. By God's grace, he has relieved me of the guilt that the trouble he found himself in wasn't my fault. But I do believe I set a terrible example for him. In my pursuit of living life my way, I only saw the present moment and failed to discern the future I was headed toward. Never believe the lie that your life doesn't affect others. It most certainly does. The people you are connected to are God-ordained; they are not for your amusement but for you to influence. Our purpose is to impact souls, and the example you set can and will affect those who are watching you. I set a terrible example for Ben, and I'm so sorry. I love my brother and I praise God for Ben's transformation and his fire for Christ now, but we both ended up in need of much healing.

In this life, each choice will lead to many roads and paths. That night, in an empty bathroom, as I was preparing for the party, I found myself rehearsing all my failures and all my pain. In a public place, a bathroom can be a fun space. It's amazing how nine girls can squeeze into a tiny little restroom! But at home unaccompanied, a bathroom can be cold and lonely. For the first time, I was getting ready by myself. No one called me. I decided to skip the pre-party and just meet up with everyone at the club. My mini skirt was blue that night. It hugged me in all the right places, giving the illusion that I had curves. The bathroom was quiet, but I couldn't distract myself from the sad memories of bad choices and friendships lost. Michael[*], my college boyfriend, was not the first person I had lost to violence. By the age of twenty-two, I had lost three other friends at such tender ages. The coping skills I had learned in counseling weren't working for me that night. Taking my heels off, I remember staring at myself in the bathroom mirror with hands pressed against the rigid countertop. My eyes began to tear up profusely. One by one, silent tears fell in place of words of which I was too broken to speak. Mascara leaked down my cheeks like rain; and in that moment, when hope seemed impossible, I spoke to God. I did not expect an answer. It was my last resort—a sign of utter desperation and emptiness. And in the space between a thought and a prayer, He heard me, and I heard Him. In my heart of hearts God answered my deepest question, "God, where were You?"

As I look back, I realize that loneliness lay behind all of my wrong choices. I wanted to belong so badly. I wanted to feel important and special in the eyes of others. Loneliness led me down a difficult path and into a terrain of emptiness. I assumed that God had left me, too. But in my state of dejection and frustration, coupled with hurt and disappointment, I cried out for Him! "Where were You?" I asked. And He answered in a most tender way. I heard from Jesus that night, and my life has never been the same.

---

* In efforts to respect his family, I have chosen to use his middle name.

The Change

Sometimes life will put you in the bathroom with all its uncomfortable smells and dirty things. But in the grime of life, you can receive grace, even in the bathroom! You can find water for cleansing from all the filth that brought you there in the first place. Jesus told the Samaritan woman, "I have living water for you" (John 4:10). He offers us the same. It's in our dirty places where we find the most need for Jesus. He invites us to call on Him for His cleansing power! So often we believe the lie that we must "fix" ourselves in order to "get right" with God. We think we have to become better people—"good girls"—by changing this first or cleaning that up. We believe we have to stop doing this or stop doing that. But in reality, God isn't moved by someone who can clean themselves up on the outside. He is more interested in those who long to be cleansed from the inside. A change of heart and mind requires a desire for God. It's the desire for Jesus that changes our lives and the results are both mysterious and very obvious.

Because of my parents and their ministry, I found myself in many religious conversations in college. My peers assumed I was a good source of information on God, but I wasn't. Some of my answers, I would make up! I didn't really know what I was talking about because I didn't really know God. I mimicked things my mom had said or I would roughly quote scriptures I'd heard my dad use in sermons. During one of these conversations, a friend told me, "It never works if you try to change too quickly. People always go back to partying even when they try hard to get back into church. It doesn't stick until you're older."

At the time, I wasn't sure what to make of what he said. Of course, I'm paraphrasing his exact words, but his thinking is actually how so many of us once believed. "God is for the old and unable", some say. "Youth is for mistakes and trial and error", our culture tells us, but this couldn't be further from the truth. It's not being older that makes turning to God "stick", it's being patient with yourself as God works. Whether we are eighteen or eighty-one, our lives can be changed by the love of God, through Jesus. Our ages have nothing to do with it. We can't approach living for God as a goal like losing weight or making better grades. Those are all attainable through self-effort. Living for the Lord requires patient trust in the process He takes us through to change our hearts and reshape our lives. It's not about what *we* can do; it's about what *He* chooses to do through us. The Lord is our source for all things, John 15 tells us. Even the desire for Him must come from Him (1 John 4:19).

Whether we are in church or in the bathroom, once we are willing to hand our hearts and lives over to Christ, the process of spiritual transformation begins. Jesus is not a magician who waves away our problems and gives us perfect pixie dust. He gently makes Himself known right in the middle of our current condition, and He extends His love into all of our places of emptiness. When we acknowledge the Lord and embrace His ways, we find Him as absolute truth. We receive Him by faith. Any other approach denies the power of Christ.

A life lived for Jesus can be super hard if you are bound to natural reasoning. The Christian life requires the opposite of everything you think makes sense. It involves a denial of self-centered fulfillment, faith in what is invisible, and a trust in what is yet to come. At times, God's ways overwhelm our mind and heart because they conflict with how we have been used to living. So faith and trust in Christ are necessary and involves stepping out into what cannot always be explained. 2 Corinthians 5:7 states we must "*walk by faith, not by sight*" (NKJV).

We don't always see what God is doing, but we know He is at work. So often we have to defend our faith against the doubts of those in the world. And at times, we have to defend this faith even with ourselves. The key is to speak the truths of scripture to our own souls. We have to remember to encourage ourselves in the Lord (1 Samuel 30:6 and 2 Timothy 3:16). It's also key to remind yourself to *"trust in the Lord with all your heart and lean not to your own understanding. Acknowledge Him in all your ways, and let Him direct your paths"* (Proverbs 3:5-6 NIV). This requires the giving up of your own ways of living, which will ultimately result in the attaining of what will never die. Surrender won't always be easy, and anyone who tells you the opposite is a liar. Let me say that again: living for Jesus is not always easy. But it is worth it! Christianity is an adventure every step of the way as you partake in a beauty that transcends human attempts at perfection. The changes that arise once we give our lives to Jesus are not immediate, but they are eternal and eventually become quite evident.

Encounters

I remember so clearly that bathroom encounter where I hit bottom of my own soul. There in that moment my sins of yesterday violently collided with my wounds and imperfections. I was overwhelmed with my lack and loneliness. Like a broken string of pearls, everything seemed to be scattering out of control. My guilt and shame closed in around me, and I was lost beyond my understanding. Though I had tried so hard to be good, I found that my sin nature had devoured me. I no longer knew the girl whom I saw in the mirror. She was a stranger to me. Her eyes were hollow and her heart was broken. It was the darkest moment of my life, but somehow Christ saw fit to make it the brightest. He chose that moment to break the silence between us and change my heart, forever.

In the book of Job Chapter 33, one of Job's friends speaks up to correct Job about his errors. Though Job was innocent in his own eyes, Elihu spoke up about seeking God in a time of trouble when there's no other alternative. It's in times of crisis that people find they need God. Elihu says in verses 26-30 about a soul who has experienced God's rescue:

> *"Then that person can pray to God and find favor with him, they will see God's face and shout for joy; he will restore them to full well-being. And they will go to others and say, 'I have sinned, I have perverted what is right, but I did not get what I deserved. God has delivered me from going down to the pit, and I shall live to enjoy the light of life.' "God does all these things to a person— twice, even three times—to turn them back from the pit, so that the light of life may shine on them"* (NIV).

I love the last portion of that passage: *"So that the light of life may shine on them."* How true this is! Jesus is *"the way, the truth and the life"* as it says in John 14:6 (NKJV). His presence illuminates our hearts and unfolds the path that will fulfill our lives. Without Jesus, we do not know which way to go. At best, we are just stumbling around, trying this thing then that thing. We hope for this relationship and desire that job. We move to this city and change that group of friends for another. None of these actions satisfy. None of these choices make good on the promise of a happier life. None of what we find outside of God is ever good enough. When we go our own way, we find ourselves running to and fro—feeling dizzy from the constant back and forth.

Such is life lived on our own. And eventually, without the Lord as our guide, we will crash into someone or something. We're never prepared for the impact. But God always extends grace in the midst of the collision.

When we look back over our lives, even though we may still be young, if we are honest with ourselves, we can note many encounters where God's love has protected us from experiencing what we truly deserved. When we pray, we open up our hearts to receive from God all the love and goodness we were searching for all along. But even when we've not yet prayed, God is still good! Our times of misery aren't a reflection of His absence from our lives; instead, these times result from our pulling away from Him. He is not to be blamed. Out of pride, it's easy to accuse Him for our troubles, but in our humility we must see that He has loved us all along.

In my hour of need, I began to see that God had covered me even in my sin. Sprinkled throughout my years of refusing Him were many mini-encounters with His love, mercy, and favor. I didn't recognize it at the time, but He kept saving me, again and again. God delivered me from a physical pit because He desired to save me from a spiritual one. He's done the same for you; and if you can't recall a rescue encounter, ask Him to show you incidents of His rescue. I promise you, you'll see them. The fact that you are here reading this book is because your life has been spared from something at one time or another. You are alive! You are here! We've had friends who weren't given the gift of turning age twenty-one, twenty-five, or thirty-three. We know people in our families or in our circles of close friends who died young. Our lives have been spared because of God's grace and mercy! The enemy desires to destroy you and prevent you from encountering God's love and finding freedom in Christ. But God has sent Jesus to rescue you!

Everyone has been blessed to encounter God in one way or another, regardless of whether they recognize the full blessing or not.

I wish I could tell you that after my bathroom prayer, I changed clothes, opened up my Bible and became a super Christian over night. As I'm typing, I'm smiling because that is the exact opposite of what really happened. Yes, I heard from God. The voice was still and small, but the answer was undeniably real. "I was with you," He spoke to my heart. This was His answer. Though this encounter happened eight years ago, I still get little chills thinking about that simple answer from a mighty God: "Katrina, I was with you."

All along I was never alone. In the crowds, I felt overlooked, but Jesus saw me. In my friendships, I felt misunderstood, but Jesus discerned my heart. In my sloppy relationships, Christ took pity and offered me His wild and glorious love. Yes, I encountered God on numerous occasions unbeknownst to me. I now reflect on moments of danger where I emerged unscathed. I remember times of recklessness when I jumped into cars with strangers and trusted my life to drunk drivers. I recall the time my car hydroplaned during a storm on the interstate; I spun out of control and slid across four lanes, yet I never crashed. I remember the news report of my fallen boyfriend who had been robbed and shot nine times only a few hours after we parted ways. I remember going to bad parties and almost getting kicked out of school for being in the wrong place at the wrong time. By God's grace, I graduated with a Bachelor's degree, first in my family, with my dignity still intact.

Yes, God had been with me through it all. His loving kindness protected me. And that night, in the bathroom, I received Him into my heart. I completely emptied myself of all my pride, anger and sorrow in the presence of God's holy love. It doesn't take a church service to save you. You don't need a pastor present to encounter God. God isn't confined to buildings and services. His Holy Spirit is alive and active and moving and cannot be contained! I love Psalms 34:6, *"In my desperation I prayed, and the Lord listened; He saved me from all my troubles"* (NLT).

The key word is "desperation." Sometimes desperation activates our point of turning to God. The Lord is not repulsed by our desperate cries. Scripture is filled with many passages that speak of God's desire to answer our prayers and deliver us from our troubles. Even if we have been unfaithful, He is always faithful. And He has promised to be our rescuer! His response to our need is not based on what we were like yesterday; His response is based on our heart's desire for Him now.

I didn't have all the fancy words for a prayer that night. I just had a mere, "Jesus, I'm so sorry. Please love me. Please forgive me." And I meant it. I truly did. But, in the bathroom that night, after my encounter with God, and after my prayer and the silence that followed, I didn't know what else to do, so I put my shoes back on, wiped my face and went to that party anyway. A transformation in our hearts does not necessarily come instantly, but a heartfelt prayer and the acceptance of God's love starts the process in motion.

Questions for Discussion

1. You've read "In many cases, it takes the brokenness of our very soul to bring us to God." Consider a time in your life when brokenness activated a desire for the Lord. Looking back, how was this brokenness necessary for the development of your relationship with Christ?

2. In this chapter we read, "Our times of misery aren't a reflection of His absence from our lives; instead, these times result from our pulling away from Him." Has this been your experience? Reflect on a past situation, and consider how God's love still kept you even in the midst of a difficult time.

3. Please reflect on the Scripture verse in Psalm 34:6. Write it in the space below.

   "Even if we have been unfaithful, He is always faithful; and He has promised to be our rescuer! His response to our need is not based on what we were like yesterday; His response is based on our heart's desire for Him now."

   Have you experienced this truth in your life? Consider how God has not based His love on your past choices but on your present desire for Him.

CHAPTER 4

Resolving Isn't Easy

They say there is purpose in God's process, and I believe that to be true. It would be a whole two years before my life began to reflect Christ. At twenty-two, I knew I'd heard from the Lord. I recognized that my sins were too many to count, and my lifestyle was keeping me from a God who loved me. I accepted the Lord and His forgiveness, but the problem was that dying to myself seemed a hard task after living easy. In spite of my new acceptance of Christ, old habits seemed to cling to me like stains.

Scripture tells us that once we receive Christ, our old life must die so that Christ's life can emerge in us and produce the character of God. In Romans 6:11, Paul writes, *"Even so consider your selves to be dead to sin, but alive to God in Christ Jesus"* (NASB). What exactly does this mean? At the time of my early walk with Jesus, I had no idea. I knew that being a Christian meant making changes, but the problem with change is that if you have not determined in your heart, change is hard to attain. The reformations Christ desires to establish within us are not based on natural reasoning or attempts to alter ourselves.

He desires to perform a spiritual transformation from the inside-out. And such a work is made possible only when we agree with His word and align ourselves to live in accordance with it. It's what the Bible calls "resolve."

In the book of Daniel, we are introduced to the young man Daniel—the book's namesake. He was positioned to make a choice: either honor God with his obedience or participate in pleasures that would dishonor the Lord. On the one hand, Daniel knew that if he chose to indulge in the pleasures surrounding him, he could do so, and still be loved by God. However, such compromise would cost him his close relationship with the Lord, as well as the great future that God had in store for him. Sound familiar?

Almost every day, we are put in this same position. The lure of doing what is socially acceptable pulls at our hearts and challenges us to forego the changes that Christ desires to produce in us. Daniel was so young, yet he knew what was at stake. He valued his relationship with God far above any popular activity, fleeting attention, or fame. So instead of compromising with the society around him, the Bible says that Daniel "*resolved*" not to defile himself during his time in Babylon. Daniel 1:8 in another translation uses the phrase, "*purposed in his heart*" (KJV).

Integrity of the Heart

I had a college friend who would proudly declare that every time she had sex, she repented immediately afterward. She would say this often and I thought it a very peculiar thing to say. I wasn't living a Christian life at all during this time of my life, but I knew something about that statement wasn't quite right. To repent means to turn away and not repeat. Yet, so many of us still hold to the mindset of thinking we can make whatever decisions we want on the premise that we can simply ask God's forgiveness following any deed. Keeping this attitude abuses God's goodness and is a manipulation of His love and kindness. If I am habitually doing things that are wrong according to what the Holy Spirit has said, either through scripture, a sermon, or personal conviction, then I have not repented. The problem with habitual sin is that no resolve has taken place. And where there is no resolve, there are no grounds for transformation. The goal of our lives is to be changed by God, so we can live lives which exhibit His supernatural goodness. The ongoing practice of sin does not produce the goodness of God. Paul speaks about this in Romans: "*What then shall we say? Shall we continue in sin so that grace may increase? By no means! How can we who died to sin live in it any longer*" (Romans 6:1-2 NASB).

Integrity of the heart results from our resolve in God. True repentance is not just asking for forgiveness; it's also saying, "yes" to a change of heart. This heart decision is resolving not to sin. It doesn't mean that we won't sin, but it does mean that we desire obedience over disobedience. The Bible explains to us that repentance means to turn from our sins and wrongdoings and let the light from God's Word remove the sinful desire of doing what is not pleasing to Christ. Of course, desiring never to sin again and actually not sinning again isn't an effortless task. We have to "*work out our salvation*" in the grace and power of God (Philippians 2:12 NASB), which means that moment by moment, we invite God to have access to our hearts. When we struggle in our own strength to remove our natural disposition to sin, we frequently fail. Romans 7:19 describes such struggle: "*For the good that I want, I do not do, but I practice the very evil that I do not want*"(NASB). Christ came to die because we are incapable of the personal transformation that God requires. Each of us is guilty of sins—both intentional and accidental. There are times where we experience remorse over our mistakes and failings and genuinely desire to never practice sin again; but our desires and our ability are two different things. Many times we fail to invite Christ's power over our temptations, so we struggle alone to overcome sin. Because our souls are not yet fully restored and we carry spiritual weaknesses in our hearts, we fail to carry out repentance perfectly. Yet even in those moments, God's love is still there for us. Because He is good and kind, He sent Jesus to dwell in us! Because of His grace and mercy, we are able to come to Him as often as we need to receive the forgiveness promised in Christ. His grace brings us into His holy transformation.

Please don't mistake resolve as being synonymous with willpower or self-determination. It's not the same, because we can never rely on our own strength. *"We can do nothing apart from Christ,"* John 15:5 declares. Resolving is simply leaning our hearts and minds into God's truth and letting Him take control. When we resolve to live our lives for Christ and set our minds on His kingdom, we'll no longer entertain or participate in things that hinder our relationship with the Lord. These things include friendships, social settings, media, and anything else that may influence us in ways contrary to Christ. Such areas cause us to fumble in our hearts and eventually in our very lives. We want Christ and His blessings, but sometimes it's so hard to give up what we've enjoyed from the world. But consider Daniel. He was taken to Babylon along with His neighbors, cousins, classmates, and friends. He saw boys from his community making choices that dishonored God. He could have joined in for friendship's sake. However, he chose to devote himself to pleasing God. Out of the entire community of young Jewish men who were captured, only Daniel and his three companions received commendation for their faithfulness to God. The Word acknowledges the faith of Daniel who faced the lions and Shadrach, Meshach, and Abednego who walked with God in the fiery furnace. Everyone else faded away in their compromises. They were unnamed and forgotten.

Show me your friends, and I'll show you your future. The four men in the book of Daniel made an impact not by going along with the crowd but by acting contrary to the crowd. Their choices for God opened doors of destiny and produced a spiritual legacy, which we are still celebrating today! The company we let influence us must reflect our resolve if we have intentions of moving forward in our relationship with Christ. Daniel and his companions possessed the integrity to do what honored God even in the midst of others who didn't. As a result, they saw and did the miraculous! Carnal choices produce carnal outcomes, and many of us, for fear of losing friendships, are living carnal lives—lives that lack integrity and void of the spiritual greatness that God desires for us. Friendship is a beautiful gift, but we can't allow it to wedge in between us and our relationship with Christ. Does this mean we cut all ties to friendships from our past? Not at all. Our old friends need to see Christ in us! We should be giving our families and friends a front row seat to watch the transformation that God is bringing about in our lives. But we must be careful not to invest ourselves in any relationship which would cause us to waver in our resolve to follow Jesus. Who and what we connect ourselves to will have major influence on our final destination. *"Do not be deceived: 'Bad company corrupts good morals,'"* 1 Corinthians 15:33 states (NASB). We want to be influencers for God's kingdom, rather than apathetically following the crowd around us, sacrificing our resolve and integrity in the process.

Replacing

As I strived in my own strength to live my new life in Christ, I made a lot of mistakes. Of course, I still do, but the difference was that I was trying so hard because my focus was still on myself. I wanted so badly to "get it right this time." Perhaps I felt as if I had something to prove. The last semester of my senior year, I did absolutely nothing. I didn't go to one single party or date or do much of anything. My friends had distanced themselves from me, so I moved back home. I didn't go anywhere; I didn't do anything. Nada. I was trying to avoid temptations that I thought would make me mess up. My dad is a pastor, and I was constantly in church or in my dad's office reading books on theology and memorizing scripture. I didn't want to be a hypocrite. I wanted to be a "real" Christian this time. So I'd go to class, stop by church, post a scripture on my Facebook page, and then go home. I'd get a coffee with my brother and talk to my cousin Jazzie on the phone. I'd help my mom and try to soak up all of her wisdom. I wanted a new routine. The few invitations I did receive, I turned them down. I thought I was guarding myself from trouble, but in reality I was only isolating my heart from living in freedom. I thought I was being devout. And I thought I was keeping temptations away. This lasted a few months, and then I met—umm "Venny." (It's a made up name, but just go with me here.) "Venny" was cool. He had swagger and was highly motivated. He was not a Believer, so needless to say, he messed up my scripture reading routine. Within a few months, I started compromising in my decisions. Again.

"What is wrong with you?" I would scold myself all the time. Mine was a frustrating situation because I knew better. Conviction is a gift, and the Holy Spirit convicts those He loves because it urges us to seek needed change. (Lord, thank you for your deliverance!)

That relationship was such a messed up situation. My loves, don't be surprised when a "Venny" shows up in the midst of your pursuit of Christ. In fact, I'd say, just expect this. "Venny" might be an actual man for you or "Venny" could be the temptations of material gain from personal opportunities that will distract you from Christ. This is normal. It's the enemy, and he tries it. He's always trying us, but he won't win. Christ won't allow him to win. Victory over temptation doesn't come from dodging bullets, but from resisting the natural urge to compromise. The problem, though, is that cutting out all things won't protect us from falling. I thought that if I isolated myself and pulled away from potential interferences, I'd stay safe from making bad choices. Dropping out is a common mistake. Isolation doesn't produce resolve; it only leaves you susceptible to other distractions like "Venny." It's not enough to just cut things out and cut people off. We have to replace what we renounce with the things of God and people of God.

I am a proud member of Pearls of Hope Outreach. We are a nonprofit organization out of North Carolina where we serve as mentors and accountability partners for young women. We do Bible studies and local outreach and really have a great time! At every meeting and event, I am amazed at the amount of encouragement I receive from these sweet friends! Ariel, one of our "Pearls," used a great analogy in our Bible studies about the need to renounce and replace. She shared with us from Matthew 12 and reminded us of what Jesus said about what happens when we don't allow God to replace the things we cast out. Verses 43-45 say:

"Now when the unclean spirit goes out of a man, it passes through waterless places seeking rest, and does not find it. Then

> *it says, 'I will return to my house from which I came'; and when it comes, it finds it [the person] unoccupied, swept, and put in order. Then it goes and takes along with it seven other spirits more wicked than itself, and they go in and live there; and the last state of that man becomes worse than the first. That is the way it will also be with this evil generation"* (NASB).

"Y'all, we've got to replace the "ratchetness" with Godliness!" Ariel says. (I just love her!) Basically what this means is, if we fail to invest in this new life we have in Christ, we'll be susceptible to temptation because our lives will be empty. Boredom is a weapon the enemy brings against us! There was nothing wrong with my going to church four nights a week or reading from my dad's Christian library, but I wasn't doing those things because I enjoyed them. Truth is, I was doing those things because I thought that's what Christians do! Did I learn a lot? Yes, I did! I was hungry for God's Word, but I made the time into tedious work, and work is boring. I was bored, and I had nothing to invest myself in that would edify me as a person and encourage me into who God was creating me to be. I love fashion, and I love movies. I love ice cream and talking on the phone and eating out and riding horses and meeting new people. And I love to travel and write and read and paint. But I had stopped all of that. I was afraid to go to the movies because I didn't want to run into anyone or see anything that might not be Christ-like. Not every movie is bad; I could have watched something decent. I didn't have to avoid *all* movies. I was scared to travel because I didn't want to be tempted to go to the clubs in my favorite cities. But clubs aren't the only entertainment. I could have gone to a play or tried out local restaurants. I could have invited my cousins to come enjoy sightseeing with me. At the time, I didn't have a large group of girlfriends whom I could call up on the phone, but I could have joined a small group at church and made new friends.

In all honesty, I was afraid I couldn't maintain my new lifestyle. I wasn't depending on God's love and goodness to keep me. I wasn't depending on Christ as my source. I was depending on myself, and this reliance on self gave way to fear. Fear is what drove me to retreat from life and others. I was afraid that I would mess up and look stupid in front of all my old friends who were more than aware of the new life I was attempting to live. I wasn't trusting God to guard me. I was trusting in Katrina. But I have learned that fear is not synonymous with resolution. Isolation is not protection from temptation. Trusting God is the only true guard that we have against falling and failing. Will we mess up? Sometimes. But I believe in the scriptures that remind us to trust in the Lord and lean on His grace!

> *"Delight yourself in the Lord, and He will give you the desires of your heart. Commit your way to the Lord; trust also in Him, and He will do it"* (Psalm 37:4-5 NASB).

Trusting God means believing He will lead, guide and equip us right in our moments of renouncing those things that tempt us to compromise. We don't have to live isolated or boring lives. We have the King of the universe living inside our hearts. There is nothing boring about that! We are called to be true lights in the world, Matthew 5:14 declares. Lights are attractive, exciting, and wonderful! Our lives are on display, whether we are aware of this or not. But if we hide our light by retreating, then we become ineffective in attracting others to Christ. Hiding is unproductive. We aren't called to hide; we are called to shine! As we trust the Lord to show us what to renounce and replace in our lives, we can trust Him to fill us with His blessings and benefits.

Fulfilled

No one likes to feel incomplete. I think that's why there are some single women, both Christian and non- Christian, who are so obsessed with relationships. We seek outside resources to fill us up without realizing that true fulfillment begins on the inside with God. Compromising happens when we search outside of Christ for things we think will make us feel complete. Compromise results from attempts to gain happiness and fulfillment on our own. We begin reaching for things instead of reaching for God. But there is nothing in creation or in anything that will ever be created which can fulfill the longings of our hearts. There is nothing outside of Christ, which satisfies. When we replace what we renounce with things that are spiritually productive and pleasing to God, we find we are so very fulfilled because all that God has for us is good. His gifts are eternal, and His ways are rewarding. When we look to God for joy and love and depend on Him to produce His goodness within us, we won't have regrets.

Scripture tells us, *"He will keep in perfect peace all those who trust in him, whose thoughts turn often to the Lord"* (Isaiah 26:3 TLB). We are instructed to keep our focus on Christ. Don't we experience the opposite of peace when we compromise? We become restless. When we make choices outside of Christ, our hearts get filled with worry, doubt, fear, and shame. We worry about someone finding out we lied. We worry about getting pregnant. We doubt our relationships and fear losing our friends. We feel ashamed when people see our pretenses, and we get embarrassed when the consequences expose us. Worry and fear are not at all fulfilling. God has a better way!

When I finally came to terms with ending things with "Venny", I felt a relief! The ties of compromise were binding, but the peace that followed obedience was liberating. Christ desires to liberate us all! This is only accomplished when we make choices to obey. Instead of dating irresponsibly, why not invest your time and effort into people who will encourage you in your new direction for Christ? And what about music? Believe it or not, music plays a huge role in our personal lives, our desires, thoughts, and choices. Instead of listening to music that encourages us to live outside of God's Word, we can replace it with worship music or Christian Rap or other contemporary Christian music. Who doesn't love Bethel, Hillsong, Jesus Culture or the 116 Crew? What about Tasha Cobbs or Travis Greene, Christon Gray or the Newsboys? All music has a message. What is the music you are listening to teaching you?

Rather than going to the clubs to be seen and noticed, play the host and invite others into your home for fellowship. Why not get involved in Bible studies with other believers and create meaningful friendships that will propel you on your journey? There you will find genuine intimacy. A friend who encourages you to compromise is not a friend. Invest your heart in people who understand your love for Christ and who will support you and pray with you as you venture into a deeper, closer relationship with Jesus. Yes, we are called to love everyone, but not everyone is meant to play an intimate part in our lives. Friendships are intimate relationships. Be sure they are building up your new heart in Christ and not tearing it down. When we find ourselves struggling between pleasing people and pleasing God, then we know that such relationships need to be replaced. We don't have to discard the person; we just need to redirect ourselves from under their influence and replace this undertow with the influence of those who will come alongside us and invest in our pursuit of Christ.

There are so many things to explore and try in this life! You can live in perfect peace! There are many fulfilling roles only you can play in God's kingdom. Don't be afraid to explore all the wonders that God has for you! Pick up that hobby that you always wanted to try. Plan a trip with friends and travel. Volunteer. Celebrate someone else's achievements. Read a great book. Even fall in love! If we are honest, once we start renouncing the things that are not Christ-like, we will admit they weren't much fun anyway, and their consequences certainly weren't worth it. I don't know about you, but I'd rather make choices that result in reward! We are unlimited in this life with Christ! In fact, we have more freedom than those in the world, because a guiltless life doesn't weigh a soul down.

Trust and Obey

As we start resolving, renouncing, and replacing, we begin operating outside of our own limited power. We simply come into agreement with the Word of God by setting our hearts to obey the truths of scripture by trusting His process. As we trust, we grow, and as we grow, we shine! Our obedience to God's Word is a reflection of our love for Him. *"If you love me, you will keep my commandments,"* John 14:15 (NASB).

Compromise is the opposite of obedience. It's a sign of distrust and doubt, which we can struggle with from time to time. But God is still good, even when we doubt, and He invites us to believe Him at His word. We can resolve in our hearts to trust the Lord in each and every area of our lives, so we can find the fulfillment that only He can give. We can take in the Word as truth for each day and overcome unbelief as God tells us, "*faith comes by hearing, and hearing by the word of God*" (Romans 10:17 NKJV). Do you believe that God's plans for you are better than anyone else's, even better than your own? If your answer is "yes," then you have great faith. If your answer is "no," then you are honest that you've had problems believing. So have I. But there is nothing too difficult for God. "*For no word from God will ever fail,*" Luke 1:37 assures us (NIV).

Obeying and resolving aren't always easy, but the results are incomparable. When we obey we trust by recognizing that our resolutions have no power outside of the strength of the Holy Spirit. Our obedience and trust can rest in the knowledge that God's plans and His promises are true and that any choices made outside of His Word will not bring blessings to our lives.

There is a song my mom sings: "*Trust and obey, for there's no other way, to be happy in Jesus, but to trust and obey*". Once we agree upon these truths—we can begin walking with a true heart of resolution. And such resolve will propel us into God's process of transformation to perfect us. No matter who you are or where you are going, it's never too late to embrace God's love for you and start seeing yourself through His eyes! No, you are not perfect, but He is perfectly able to perfect you in Christ. He is creating you in the image of Jesus. You can know His love as you become all He has created you to be. Just trust and obey!

Resolving reflects the change of direction in our lives, and that new direction requires vision. Those with no vision for the future eventually revert to old habits of the past. I've seen it happen, and so have you. I've been guilty of reverting backward a time or two, and so have you. Why is this? Well, it's because we have no vision outside of Christ. Psalm 119:105 teaches, "*Your words are a light to the path ahead of me and keep me from stumbling"* (TLB). We can't see what God sees! He sees in hidden places, Jeremiah 23:24 tells us, so we must trust Him through His word, because it reveals His love and goodness! We renounce the things that hinder us from intimacy with Him, because we know that our hearts are only made alive in Jesus! So, we resolve, renounce, and replace because we love our God and we can trust that His love will never leave us empty.

In this journey with Jesus, we have options for joy! As the Lord leads us, He opens our eyes to all the wonders and blessings that He alone can bring. Our lives in Christ don't have to be flat and one-dimensional. In Christ there are depths and heights. Through His love, we find purpose and adventure. There is rich fulfillment in the Lord, but it starts with trusting that He is good by obeying His word. Nothing else will bring us peace and satisfaction: not our boyfriends or our husbands, or our carriers or friendships. It's God whom we're made for. He is our source for every good thing we hope to attain. It's not our makeup, our curves, or our swagger that makes us whole. These things aren't sinful in and of themselves, but they will never ever fulfill us.

In my early walk with Christ, I wasn't aware that I wasn't trusting in God, but I was very aware I was not fulfilled. I kept trying and trying and then, because I was operating from my own strength, I got drained and lonely and bored. There were many avenues that I could have taken in Christ, but I didn't explore very many of them because I wasn't trusting in the Lord. I wasn't seeking His wisdom. I had emptied myself of so much, but I never allowed Him the opportunity to replace any of it. So when "Venny" came along, I lost my determination to pursue Christ for a few months. That experience only filled me up with hot air. There was no substance to it, and eventually it deflated and left me with nothing. So what did I do? I turned to the One who could restore me. With a humbled heart I prayed, "Lord, I'm back. I messed up again, and I'm so sorry. Please give me a new heart."

Upon my undergraduate graduation and after many, many talks with my dad, I realized that being a Christian doesn't mean denying yourself to living life! When we replace what we renounce with the goodness that God offers us, we are never left lacking. Sometimes we might feel uncomfortable, uncertain, or out of place, but we never experience regret or feel used. Resolving is not easy because it brings us to places where our old fleshly lives war with our new spiritual lives in Christ. Galatians 5:17 states, *"These two forces within us are constantly fighting each other to win control over us"* (TLB). This new life seems opposite of what makes sense to the natural mind, and others around us might not understand, but Christ sees us and He understands! He's the only one who knows what He's doing. He knows us better than we know ourselves, so we can trust His process of perfection within us. He alone knows what is best for His daughters, and His supernatural ways are beautiful. He came to fill our lives! He is a gift, and He gives us gifts continually! His ways are trustworthy and His plans for us are good. They involve replacing our temptations and compromise with His joy, peace, freedom, love, and creativity! Jesus is exciting, and He invites us to explore Him in all things! Christ came to give us abundant life! So honey, dare to live! Work, Pray, Slay! And do it all to the glory of God (1 Corinthians 10:31).

Questions for Discussion

1. Scripture tells us that once we receive Christ, our old self must die so that Christ's life can emerge in us and produce the character of God. Please record Romans 6:11 in the space below.

   Does this Scripture reflect your current relationship with Jesus?

2. You've read, "The goal of our lives is to be changed by God, so we can live lives which produce His supernatural goodness." How does this goal conflict with the world's goals for our lives? Have you ever experienced a collision between what the world wants for you and what God desires? Please explain.

3. '*If you love me, you will keep my commandments,*' John 14:15 says (NASB).

   Consider a time when it was particularly difficult for you to be obedient to God. What was the outcome of your obedience? What do you think would have resulted had you chosen to compromise? In what ways did your obedience to God bring you closer to His love and goodness?

CHAPTER 5

Combatting Our Compromise

One of the undeniable struggles in living in liberty and confidence in Christ stems from placing more focus on what others think of us rather than on what God thinks and what scripture teaches. In my experience, this has been one of the greatest hindrances to fully living, loving, and enjoying freedom in my relationship with Christ. When we perform for others instead of pleasing Jesus, we cheat ourselves out of heavenly rewards. Even in communities of faith, there are many of us who wear masks to conceal the truth of who we are in efforts to appease others or to satisfy our own selfishness. This is compromise, which is comprised of concealed truths and denial. But when we open up our hearts to the Lord, we find freedom from hiding and rest from pretenses. God is calling us to be authentic. He does not want just pieces of us. He invites us to live "out loud" in confidence and high esteem, not in hiding or in dishonesty. Otherwise, the enemy will begin to lay traps of compromise in the darkness of our half-truths. Fungus grows in the darkness, but we are to shine the light of Christ without shame.

Being transparent is hard though, isn't it? Many of us feel caught between an identity of who we think we should be and who God has called us to be. We are intimidated to be open, for fear that someone will see our scars and find us unlovely. But Christ's love gives us freedom from those pressures and fears. You see, none of us are beautiful outside of Him. So He invites each of us to remove our masks of compromise and false identities. He's not afraid of what we are struggling with and He desires that we don't hold back. He alone understands our thoughts and every care. We can trust Him in His mission to cultivate authenticity within us all! But when we take our eyes off of the Lord and begin to seek validation from other people or other things, compromise occurs. By questioning His truth about who we are and how we are meant to live, we exchange our freedom for lies, and we enter into fabrications of selfish determination. It always starts with small adjustments here and there—subtle excuses or disguised unbelief. We accept lies because we don't believe the truth will set us free. We give our love away before marriage because we believe the excuse that waiting is not practical or possible any more. We cut corners in the workplace to get ahead, because the world tells us that integrity doesn't always guarantee promotions.

Our society proclaims one thing, while scripture tells us another, and we go back and forth in uncertainty over whose voice to follow. There are so many choices to make in this life, but if our decisions aren't improving our relationship with Christ, they will eventually strain it. That's the objective of compromise. It's a tool of the enemy to distance you from an intimate relationship with the Lord and lead you out from underneath the peace and protection of God. The devil works to take away your security and faith in Christ and rob you of your influence in this dark world. We cannot forget that Christ has entrusted us with His Gospel! We are freedom message-bearers! We have the answers the world is seeking in their very souls, but if our lives look like theirs, we only further them in their spiritual blindness as well as in our own.

A few summers ago, I had the pleasure of spending some time with a young lady, who needed a lot of advice. She desired an understanding of Christianity, but struggled in matters of the heart. Many times, she'd share with me how she and her boyfriend would sleep in the same bed together, without temptation, but couldn't understand why she felt so numb in her prayer life.

"You've conditioned yourself to be comfortable in compromising, so how do you expect to hear from the Lord", I asked her one day, "Why do you expect to hear from Him in prayer, when you are ignoring Him in your choices"?

We are surrounded by all sorts of temptations in our lives. We can't expect to combat these persuasive lies when we choose to toy with them. Compromise desensitizes us from the pull and influence of the Holy Spirit. It's the subtle choices that we excuse and the thoughts we entertain that serve as traps to lead us astray from God's presence. The more we play with compromise, the less we are able to discern the instructions of the Holy Spirit. A lack of spiritual sensitivity is why some of us can sin and not "feel bad." Of course, we know that obedience is not based on feelings or emotions, but we *should* be concerned when we have done something that isn't right. Conviction is a gift. It's a spiritual guardrail intended to keep us from falling off the cliff, yet even in our salvation, some of us have fallen into pits simply because we had no discernment or conviction due to habitual compromise.

Sweet Confessions

Friends, when we honor the Lord, He will guard us and protect us. Compromising creates callouses over our hearts; it prevents us from repentance and confession. It's all the working of the enemy of our souls. He can't steal your salvation, but if he can get you to a place where you are no longer concerned about repenting and confessing, then he can fool you into believing that you don't need forgiveness. This is not liberation; it's spiritual destruction and sabotage. How can we expect to live in fullness if we are not forgiven and how can we receive forgiveness if we don't request it?

> *"If we confess our sins, He is faithful and just and will forgive us our sins and purify us from all unrighteousness,"* 1 John 1:9 declares (NIV).

Compromise distracts us from confession, and we *need* to confess. And often! "Y.O.L.O." has no place in the heart of a Believer. This is not the attitude of a repentant heart whose desires are for freedom through confession. The infamous motto, "You only live once" has beckoned us to make choices in the here and now that hinder our freedom and our futures. In reckless abandon, so many of us have experienced devastation due to choices made without regarding the future consequences. Such have placed a toll on our hearts and on our souls. "Y.O.L.O." is a lie. There is a life after this one and a God who will hold us accountable for every choice that we make here on earth (Romans 2: 16 NIV). As Christians, we ought to be living in preparation for eternity, not in hiding due to our carnal choices, intentionally made in this life.

Repentance requires humility, and confession helps fashion in us the freedom of forgiveness. God's forgiveness precedes our purity, and it's required for receiving salvation in the first place. "No regrets" is not the anthem of a believer. There will be mistakes and bad choices that we make along the way. Why? Because we are human. We are flawed and imperfect, so humility and our love for our Savior beacons us to admit this truth through confession and repentance. We cannot receive forgiveness for things we are not sorrowful over. Yes, you are always loved, but our access to God is through the forgiveness of sins bought by Christ on the cross (1 Peter 3:18). We cannot afford to make the mistake of thinking we can abuse the grace of God through habitual compromise and still be in relationship with Him.

Listen, people will always have their opinions and suggestions about what you should do, how you should do it, and when things should be done. Our world idolizes what God detests and insists that we approve of it. They demand our tolerance of sin, yet they are intolerant of our stance for holiness. This is the war that wages in this world, but we must choose sides (Luke 16:13). If those you follow aren't following Christ, beware of their advice and suggestions. "*Though they know God's decree that those who practice such things [sin] deserve to die, they not only do them but give approval to those who practice them*", Romans 1:32 (NIV).

Yes, the world pulls on us, beaconing us to compromise, but we have the choice to say, "no". The presence of the Holy Spirit is necessary if we desire to please the Lord, but compromise will surely hinder His voice. As we live for Christ, we must protect our hearts from choices that will lead us astray and from those who are determined to get us off course. A woman who is easily influenced has the company of many companions; but those who walk in integrity do so at the risk of walking alone. Yet God is with her (Psalm 46:5).

Do you know the voice of God? What does His word say to you? His approval is the only one that matters and the only one that lasts eternally. *"I alone know the plans that I have for you. They are plans for your good. My plans will produce hope and a future in you"*, God decrees in Jeremiah 29:11 (paraphrase mine).

Only God's plans for you are lasting and rooted in goodness. People's plans change. Their agendas change. Human ideas, intentions, and interests change; even their love changes and we know this to be true. In most cases, compromises are founded on self-centered interests. When your coworkers urge you to compromise, it's not because they care about your well-being. Those friends who influence you to live a life of compromise aren't doing so out of concern for your soul. That guy who urges you to go just a little further with him is not doing so because he desires to love you as Christ loves the church. I promise you, when we live our lives to please the world, we will seriously miss out on God's amazing plans for us, with nothing of eternal value to show for it.

Here are some examples to ponder:

> The professional woman who is too concerned about her reputation to stand up for honesty at a business meeting where others are manipulating the numbers for the sake of a "good deal"— she doesn't realize that she could be the very example of Christ that her coworkers need to see.
>
> The college student consumed with her friends and their idea of "fun" who chooses to live the party life instead of stepping out from the crowd—she fails to realize that her friends are truly lost. God wants to use her to shine His light into their

darkness, but she emulates her friends in order to keep their approval of her. She's become a stumbling block instead of a blessing.

The stay-at-home mom who would rather endure dirty talk and gossip with her neighbors than be impolite in their eyes—she's unaware that her participation is hurting the person across the street for whom she has promised to pray for.

The athlete who would rather share in vulgar jokes in the locker room than risk looking "lame"—she doesn't realize that the leadership opportunity that God blessed her with was intended to lead her teammates to Christ.

We will never know how others will internalize our actions. Ignorance of this does not void us of the responsibility that we have to live righteously in all circumstances. We are accountable to Christ for the example that we set for others. And though we are "grown" and have the right to do whatever we wish, this doesn't give us permission to disregard how our choices will influence those around us.

""*I have the right to do anything," you say—but not everything is beneficial. "I have the right to do anything"—but not everything is constructive*", 1 Corinthians 10:23 tells us. Yet, in our immaturity, we tend to look at our own lifestyles and our own agendas and we want those around us to adapt to our preferences. We convince ourselves that we haven't hurt anyone, but compromise never shows you the results, immediately. A mentality that is self-indulgent and self-focused will not produce the goodness of Christ in our lives. We must consider how our actions will affect others and how our choices will impact the hearts that Christ as entrusted to us.

As Christians, we must be willing to risk the displeasure of the world, our families and friends, and sometimes even that of our selves all for the sake of pleasing Christ. We must know His voice and what is truly at stake. It's not our reputation, our career, or our popularity in the world that gives us eternal life. It's Jesus. And if we belong to Him, it should be our highest joy to reflect Him in every area of life. This sort of faithfulness is necessary if we want God to use our lives for His glory! The Holy Spirit provokes change in a faithful heart, but change won't come from excuses based on our self-interests or compromises. Our excuses will excuse us from eternal rewards! The point of this life is to prepare us for the next one. Ladies, we are living for more than just a Friday night. We are living beyond the fads, above the rat race, and past this world's empty promises. When we compromise, we live out of a limited perspective—one which the Bible tells us will fade away (1 John chapter 2). The "here and now" won't last forever. Each day becomes the past, and honestly, many of us have nothing to show for the compromises made in past moments.

Ribbons and Bows

Let's say that it's your birthday and all your friends stop by to celebrate with you. As they arrive one by one, they present you with beautifully wrapped gift boxes and bags. The boxes are delicately decorated and presented to you in abundance! Is that a Kate Spade box? Oh, my!

Throughout the entire celebration, your friends give speeches about how much you mean to them and how your friendship has had such a positive influence on their lives. Some of your friends even cry as an expression of their love for you. Deep down you're touched and moved by their kindnesses. You take pictures and recount fond memories. It's a beautiful night for you!

Once the evening is over and all your guests have gone, you begin to open each expensively wrapped present. The boxes are of various sizes. Some are wrapped in gold paper while others are bound up with glitter and ruffles. You peel away the paper, box by box, only to discover that each box is empty. Piles and piles of white tissue paper line your floor. Ribbons and bows are sprawled out everywhere, and empty boxes lie open at your feet. You recall the speeches and the tears, and you sit confused. What was the point of the speeches? Why would they go through all that huffing and puffing? You notice there are some unopened cards, so you read them; but they, too, are empty—blank inside; not even one signature! What would be your reaction to such a situation? What sort of thoughts would run through your mind? What emotions would you express? I'll tell you what I'd do, I'd cry!

Sometimes as Christians we present our exterior lives just as these expensively packaged boxes with all the ribbons and bows. We look amazing from the outside! We say the right things, we attend church, and we even say a few prayers, yet our hearts and our lives and our daily expressions of worship to God can be empty.

"Barely, barely, I say unto thee," my friend Jessica Gray cries out on occasion! We all laugh at the joke, but unfortunately many people live barely lives—meagerly existing from one moment to the next. They hope their image will cover up the truth, but it's difficult to fake things and still be taken seriously. We can't be more concerned with looking the part than being the part.

"These people say they honor me, but their hearts are far away.

Their worship is worthless," Matthew 15:8-9 reads (TLB). Our actions must reflect the truths that should be stored in our souls. We find the remedy to this in Psalm 119:11: *"I have thought much about your words and stored them in my heart so that they would hold me back from sin"* (TLB).

Compromise causes us to become ineffective and results in worthless worship. Empty hearts won't make fruitful impacts. Pretend Christianity won't produce God's glory in our lives. Ladies, it's time to choose sides. The middle isn't safe ground. If anything, it is the most dangerous ground of all to stand on because it has no foundation whatsoever and will cause us to look foolish when it gives way. We've all seen this happen to other women who became victims of their own compromise. But for some reason, we think we are smart enough to fool others, fool ourselves, or even fool God. Not so! What is done in secret will eventually be brought to light, and in most cases, for everyone to see! We can make our choices, but we can't choose our consequences, as my mom would say.

Compromise entails making decisions we think we can get away with, but the truth is no one ever gets away with anything. God sees all. His Word says, *"Whoever conceals their sins does not prosper, but the one who confesses and renounces them finds mercy"* (Proverbs 28:13 NIV). This verse emphasizes confession, but in our moments of compromise, we aren't confessing. We are concealing. We don't want anyone to know, and we might even get offended if confronted by what we know is right. This attitude is not of Christ. And it's definitely not freedom.

If we begin to focus on our agendas and take on the responsibility of making our own choices over God's Word and His truth, we will sooner or later find ourselves suffering in the pains of sin's consequences. We hide in our compromise because it doesn't produce light. Sin should not be our prerogative. It is not a preference we should opt for because we know its ultimate purpose is to destroy in us the new life God desires to create. So we don't trust ourselves to fight compromise in our own strength because our hearts can deceive us. Sin is a seductress! "It always leads us further than we thought we'd go," Kay Arthur says. And how right she is! Yes, sin's agenda is to position us away from the path of eternal life in Christ by enticing us to please our flesh. So in the fight, we must trust our God to guide us in our decision-making and focus on pleasing Him rather than ourselves. Jeremiah 17:9 tells us, *"The heart is deceitful above all things and beyond cure. Who can understand it"* (NIV). Only the Lord!

We all have lived below our God-given potential. We've all made poor choices, and we all know what it's like to search for purpose and meaning outside of the Lord. Some of us went about it through education. Others used the medium of sex and relationships or success in financial exploits. We believed the illusion that we were self-sufficient. But no matter what we tried to fill ourselves up with, in the end, we were always empty without Jesus. We cannot overlook that God's love and mercy is a gift given to those who do not deserve it. No goodness is produced apart from Christ. Yes, we can go through the motions and say all the right things. We can give to the poor, pray extravagant prayers, or preach to the godless, but if we are not living our lives connected to Him as the source of love and goodness that our hearts seek, then we are just living a frilly life—a life that's unproductive for God's kingdom.

Intentions

A friend's birthday party was approaching and I was happy to receive an invitation. She was a new friend. I didn't know her very well, but I was pleased with the candle I had purchased for her. A few days before the party, in a group text, people asked her what she wanted for a gift and she mentioned she preferred gift cards because she always got scented lotion or candles that she didn't like. "Oh great," I thought as I made a mental note to take the candle back to the store and exchange it for a gift card before the party. I put the candle in the front seat of my car with the intention of taking it back, but I kept forgetting to make the exchange. On the night of the party, as I rushed home to get ready, I saw that the return date had expired on the receipt and I'd waited too late. What was I going to do? I had every intention of taking the candle back in order to get her the gift card she desired, but time had run out and I had missed my opportunity. I was stuck with a honey-flower scented candle as a gift for a person who didn't enjoy candles. My good intention had totally failed.

People in our culture mistake good intentions for some version of faithfulness. They think as long as they intend to do something, then that's what counts. Umm, no. This thinking goes against what scripture tells us. In fact, in the book of James, we are introduced to the idea that knowing the good we are to do but not doing it is a sin (James 4:17).

James goes so far as to say that the lifestyle of knowing right, yet failing to act is one of self-deception. In my opinion, this is the worst kind of lie—the lie you create and then believe. James calls us to the lifelong challenge to be "*doers of the word, and not hearers only, deceiving yourselves*" (James 1:22 NKJV). We're not to say "amen" and make promises we do not keep. We must live as "doers" with actions that come from our being in Christ—an identity intricately woven into the measure of who we are as individuals in Jesus. It's in Him that our integrity and our faithfulness are shaped.

I am Katrina. But I am a Christian first. I am a woman, but my identity in Christ must be primary. I am married, but my relationship with Christ is a priority above all others. Our loyalty must be to Him first and foremost. We must not only agree with what God's Word says, but we must act upon it. We must live it out and exemplify the heart of Christ, because that is who we are. As my brother so often reminds me, "Trina", he says, "Keep the main thing the main thing". And what is the main thing and mission of our lives? Well, it's to love and please Jesus with all that we are. That means when it's time to forgive, we forgive. When it's time to stop, we stop. When it's time to pray, we pray. When it's time to confess, we confess.

You might ask, but how do I know if my intentions are aligned with God's Word? What if I'm unaware that I'm compromising? Good questions! Scripture tells us to examine our hearts from time to time. 2 Corinthians 13:5 requires of us: *"Check up on yourselves. Are you really Christians? Do you pass the test? Do you feel Christ's presence and power more and more within you"* (TLB). Scripture urges us to check on our hearts, regularly, and in Jeremiah 17:10, God promises to do the same: *"I, the Lord, search the heart. I test the mind"* (NASB).

Each day, and as often as the Holy Spirit leads us, we should invite the Lord to examine our hearts and uncover any faults we might have. This examination takes place through actively engaging with scripture as a way of life. As we read and invite God to teach us through the pages of His word, the Holy Spirit reveals His truths and we gain understanding regarding what it means to live a life pleasing to Christ. The Bible is not just a book to reference for speeches or a place from which to gain inspiring quotes. It is alive and full of the power we need for daily confidence and holiness. Hebrews 4:12 says, *"For whatever God says to us is full of living power: it is sharper than the sharpest dagger, cutting swift and deep into our innermost thoughts and desires with all their parts, exposing us for what we really are"* (TLB). As God searches our hearts, He is looking for Himself in us. He seeks evidence of His Spirit and His Son. His love and His righteousness are what the Holy Spirit wants to establish within us. If we trust God enough to examine us, as the Psalmist requests, then He can bring forth the truth of who we really are as He sees us. The Psalmist writes: *"Search me, O God, and know my heart; Try me and know my anxious thoughts; and see if there be any hurtful way in me, and lead me in the everlasting way"* (Psalm 139: 23-24 NASB).

Through His eyes and heart, we obtain mercy, correction, and His life-changing love. His eyes are far more merciful and loving than ours are! Through our own attempts at goodness, we find such to be impossible. In the end we will always find ourselves in need of Christ. Instead of seeing how far we can get on our own, why not entrust every step to God from the start? He's the only One who knows where we are going, and He has proven Himself to be trustworthy.

As we make decisions in this life, we must allow the Holy Spirit to transform our hearts. This work is accomplished by obeying His word; not just quoting it. To obey, we must depend on God's grace through Jesus who is the Living Word within us. We must live *in* the Word and let the Word live *in* us. All of this goes beyond being good; it actually produces real holiness!

When we love God—truly love Him, we begin to combat our tendency to compromise. We no longer ask the question, "Is this a sin?" Instead, we are motivated to ask, "Will this act be pleasing to

God?" To make decisions solely based on whether or not something is or isn't a sin doesn't reflect a relationship of love with God nor a changed heart. That is religion and religion is not relationship. Loving the Lord is not about what we can or can't get away with doing. When we love God, we are consumed with what He loves. It goes beyond just saying, quoting or verbally agreeing with a verse of scripture. Rather, it is intentionally living to express Christ through willing obedience and trust that His plans and instructions are for our absolute good. This belief is faith. We can profess to believe in God or say that "Jesus died for my sins" or declare that we really do love God, but what good are such proclamations if our lives do not exemplify this truth?

As we live our lives to glorify God, we not only invite His changes, we position ourselves to combat compromise, which puts a smile on our Savior's face! Compromising reflects unbelief and a lack of faith, but our God desires to increase our faith and restore our hearts. We don't have time to live lukewarm, halfhearted, compromised lives for God. Our love for Him eliminates our leftovers, and it fills our pretty boxes with more than just pretensions and powerless words. You and I can become dynamic Christ-followers. It starts with going beyond just good intentions.

Why are You Still Struggling with That?

Just as God gives gifts, so, too, does this world. But the world's gifts are also its curses. The fun is momentary and short-lived. Eventually, we become dissatisfied and left wanting more. Each step lures us closer into the trap. And what is the trap? It's the lie that says, "you're missing out." How many of us have fallen for that lie? In our relationships, in our pursuits, in our consumption and compulsions, we fall because that's what traps do. They cause you to fall. They cause you to believe lies. So why do we still fall for the lies?

You might have heard it said that there's a partial truth with every lie, but sometimes it's the lies that dangle first. Lies can be deceitful that way; they can hide just as well in the front as they can in the back. This is why scripture warns us to guard our hearts. Proverbs 4:23 states, "*Above all else, guard your heart, for everything you do flows from it*" (NIV).

Acting in compromise is the exact opposite of guarding your heart; it's believing a lie when you know the truth. That is why we must "*trust in the Lord and lean not to our own understanding*" (Proverbs 3:5). Our world inundates us with so many messages about doing our own thing. It feels good to say it or sing it, but many of us have felt the sting produced from leaning to our own understanding by believing untruths told to us by the world. A lie can be entertaining, but it's not everlasting.

For my daughter's first birthday, someone gave us a shirt that said, "Follow your heart." I took it back and exchanged it for something else because I hate that phrase. Why am I supposed to follow my heart? Where is it going? Our hearts were made for Christ. Follow Him! Where He leads is where we will surely find ourselves—our true selves, and the abundance He has for us! When we follow our hearts, we get off course. Our hearts don't lead us to happiness and our own understanding will mislead us and get us lost every time (see Jeremiah 17:9). The emphasis on our choices can be selfish and self-centered, so when we follow our hearts, it ultimately leads to compromise.

As Believers, we are on mission to glorify God with everything we do. We are all in process, and progress requires our full participation. We cannot claim progress if we are insistent on making backward choices. We cannot expect to see the image of Christ reflected in our lives if we are continuously making worldly decisions. Nothing I'm saying is new news to most of us. We know that compromising is a danger. So, why do we still struggle with it? I dare say we entertain compromise because we are still operating in doubt that God knows what's best for us. Our compromise results from not trusting the Lord or the process He puts us through to change us and make us new. Our excuses are easier than our obedience. Our compromise seems more attractive than God's promises. But God can be trusted! He longs to expose our excuses, heal what has been unmasked, and redeem our hearts! My prayer for every one of us is that, when it is all said and done, people will recognize us as women who have been changed by Jesus! We must know God's Word in order to do God's Word; and in our obedience, our struggles begin to subside.

Compromise takes us down a slippery slope in a direction opposite of the God who loves us. Questionable choices wedge in as a wall between our confidence in Christ and our harmony with God and others. In Genesis 3, Adam and Eve hid from God after they compromised—not before. Their decision cost them far more than what they thought they would gain. Learn from their example, because sin's result is the same with us. In the moment, our compromise can seem reasonable but the delusion is only momentary. Sin's destruction multiplies in brokenness, just as it did for Adam and Eve—broken hearts, broken relationships, and broken dreams. All unnecessary. If we are honest, our compromise is never worth the consequences that come as a result.

Though we fall, Christ's love over us desires to lift us above our imperfections. It begins with confession and repentance over our compromises. It's the only way, according to the Bible, because we cannot access God without Jesus and we cannot receive Jesus without confession. Such a life won't win us many public accolades by the world's standards. Their message is the exact opposite: "Do what you want. Live how you want and refuse to change for anyone". In their lust for liberation, they refuse the power of Christ's freedom in their lives and desire to sway you, as well. Society wants nothing to do with confession because, according to scripture, they desire to live void of God's presence and holy nature (Romans 1:20-21). So, if you've been striving to win that crown and sash of honor in your social life, you might want to take a deep breath and realize that, in this life, it may never come. Your unsaved loved ones and acquaintances probably won't be on board with some of your new choices and convictions. They won't understand you because they are operating from a different spirit than the Spirit who is busy transforming you. They don't get it. They are confused about you. The Bible tells us why: *"But the natural man does not receive the things of the Spirit of God, for they are foolishness to him; nor can he know them, because they are spiritually discerned"* (1 Corinthians 2:14 NKJV).

What the world sees as foolish, God sees as honorable and pleasing; when we do His will, we bring Him glory. But compromise counteracts this. "Keep the main thing the main thing", my brother always reminds me. The main thing is pleasing Jesus, not matter what.

When we get to Heaven, we will meet millions upon millions of saints who have lived radical lives for Christ. Some lived lives on display before crowds, and others did acts of obedience and service unnoticed. Either way, whether big or small, nothing for Christ is accomplished by compromise. Let's agree to follow the great examples of other believers and live our lives for the glory of God rather than struggling for the transitory approval of others!

Swimming

No one understands you like the Lord! He understands why you do what you do, why you feel the way you feel, why you dream what you dream, and why you wrestle with the things that He alone knows. Christ understands where you are right now, and believe it or not; He hopes you will invite Him in! He will conquer your compromising heart! In Him, you have victory over your struggles, and this victory starts by discarding excuses and drawing near to the Lord. Draw near by embracing His truth and inviting the Holy Spirit to play an active role in your life.

The Bible teaches: *"No one who abides in Him keeps on sinning; no one who keeps on sinning has either seen Him or known Him"* (see 1 John 3:6). When we compromise, we walk out from underneath the covering of God's love to enjoy someone or something that seems to be more pleasing than the Lord. At this point, we are not abiding. We find ourselves left unprotected and exposed to the elements of this fallen world. We are like someone who is floating in the ocean without a raft or a life jacket. If we are not intentionally swimming toward the shore, the current will carry us further than we ever intended to go. There may be multitudes of people floating away with us, but no one person can save another. We'd all be floating toward disaster and far away from the shore and its provisions!

When we don't focus on Jesus, we will find ourselves drowning in temptation and become ineffective for the ministry to which He has called us. Such temptation isn't always external. Sometimes, it's internal and without the filling of the Holy Spirit, we are vulnerable. But Christ is our shore! With every stroke of obedience and faith toward the Lord, we draw closer and closer to Him; and we get strength to contest the opposition coming from the waves. There are sharks in the middle of the ocean! And often there is no ground to stand on. The world is in opposition to you because of Christ. They want to pull you into the depths of compromise in which they swim.

"But, I'm strong enough to handle this," you might be thinking. I argue that you're not. That's why you keep struggling and going back and forth. "But I'm still a good person," you might counter, as so many do. But scripture says only God is good (Matthew 19:17). Our flesh is weak and is not to be trusted. Matthew 26:41 cautions, *"Watch and pray, so that you do not fall into temptation: the spirit is willing, but the flesh is weak* (NIV). Yes, our flesh is weak. If it were strong, we wouldn't need a Savior. And anything we do outside of Christ is guaranteed to be in opposition to Christ. We cannot expect Godly results to come from worldly decisions. He will not bless what He's not a part of.

So where does that leave us? Well, it should lead us into a deeper faith in God. We can be "good" on our own by our own standards and our own efforts, but there is no heart change in that. Our goodness won't produce relationship with God. Only Christ can do that for us. The standards we live by will never measure up to God's holiness, and the opinions we hold within ourselves will never equal the mind of Christ. Understanding that loving Jesus is not about any goodness in us allows us to depend more on His grace in times of temptation. We can stand firmly by trusting God and handing our struggles over to Him because we know that compromising will compromise God's development in us. He is the only rock to stand on, and there is no truth outside of Him. When we compromise, we settle for what we can get instead of trusting God that we will receive all that He has promised to give.

For all of us, there will be seasons of temptation. But in those seasons, we don't have to compromise. Compromising is easy. It doesn't require the building of character, the exercise of faith, or continual transformation. But we have not been called to be easy women. Yielding to temptation doesn't have to be our reality. We don't have to rely on our ability to be "good" because our goodness is not the standard. If it were, then what would be the need for Christ? We cannot battle temptation by our good efforts or our positive affirmations. The Lord alone can keep us from falling into temptation, but we must keep our hearts and minds on Him! He is merciful and wants to aid us. He will bring us back to shore!

Be encouraged, friends, because your life is impactful! Your choices matter and the life you live is on display. Believers and non-believers are watching you. According to Hebrews 12:1, so are those Christians who have gone before you. A great cloud of witnesses surrounds you always. They are cheering you on, and they want you to be successful in your relationship with Christ and in your spiritual development here on earth. In a way, even the non-believers want to see you successful because they are looking for something authentic. They often watch the closest because they are looking for hope and reasons to believe.

Questions for Discussion

1. In this chapter, you've read, "Compromising occurs when we take our eyes off of the Lord and begin to seek validation from other people or other things." Has this been true in your experience? Reflect on times of compromise in your life and the validation you were seeking? Why were you seeking these validations? How has Christ been faithful in giving you the validation you need?

2. Please record Romans 6:20-23 in the space below.

   What is this verse saying to you? How can you apply this scripture when you are faced with the choice to compromise?

3. "It's not about any ability in yourself to be good..." It's about "the God who so radically loves us!" In what ways do these statements challenge you? Do you find yourself trying to be good on your own in various areas of your life? How can depending on God's goodness and love by abiding in Christ free you from any self-effort at goodness and the struggle and pressures of perfectionism?

CHAPTER 6

Woman to Woman

So, we're women right? And we're fabulous! Our creativity, our curves, our intellect, our mystery… we're awesome! But we're also targets and we've each fallen prey to misconceptions on so many different levels. Some of us have made the mistake that Christian girls and "good girls" are synonymous. This association is just not true. A so-called "good girl" doesn't equal a woman whose heart and mind is stayed on Christ. Being good results from personal effort; being a Christian involves a state of spiritual transformation beyond what we are able to do ourselves. It requires a relationship with God, and to be honest; He isn't looking for "good girls" to bear His name. He's looking for women with humble hearts who desire more of Him. This is the mission and the call for Christ-like living. His Holy Spirit longs to produce a change in us, which goes beyond self-improvement. God is in the process of perfecting Christ in us. He is working to produce His holiness in our lives.

Upon graduating from UNC Charlotte in 2009, I had the opportunity to move to New York to pursue a full time modeling career.

Locally, I was doing well. I was traveling out of state and making good connections. While working as a print model for a major department store, I landed a contract with a hip-hop clothing label plus a few small acting roles in movies and on TV. My agents strongly suggested that I move to New York City, but I was torn between going further in modeling and advancing my education with a Master's degree. I wanted both, but I wasn't sure which immediate choice was best. After multiple deliberations with my parents, I decided to move to Greensboro, North Carolina and go in the exact opposite direction. I'd been accepted into UNC Greensboro's graduate school, and I assured myself that fashion would be waiting for me after I completed my one and a half year-program. The first semester was terrible. As I saw my former model mates becoming successful with high-end fashion campaigns and getting to travel overseas, I regretted my decision to forego New York City. I felt like I had made the wrong choice and I became burdened with the idea that I had missed out on my dream and made a foolish mistake. With aching prayers, I asked the Lord to direct my steps into what He thought was best for me. Day by day, my studies began to take more of my attention and my longing for fashion began to subside. I met new friends at a young community church I attended, and one day, I realized that distancing myself from the fashion industry wasn't as disadvantageous as it had once seemed.

Being away from the distraction and pressures of the fashion world allowed me to focus on the new identity and character that the Lord was building in me. In Greensboro, I wasn't the pastor's daughter, no one knew of my past mistakes and no one knew me as a fashion model. I was just this new girl without any labels. I was free to explore and learn who I really was in Christ. During those three semesters, I learned to lean on God's grace to overcome my old nature. Being a stranger in a new town melted away the pressure I often felt to be perfect. Those semesters separated me from fashion, but were imperative for my personal growth and my future. Although the time out from the fashion world cost me my modeling career, in the end, I gained a confidence in Christ that has proved itself in the long run. I gained a true sense of being myself as God sees me. I didn't understand at the time, but God was setting me up to depend on His abilities and not my own. He was teaching me and conditioning me to lay aside what I thought was good for me, so that He could create His goodness within me.

God's love is immeasurable. We don't always recognize His hand moving on our behalf, but rest assured, He is at work in us, and all around us. Even when we find ourselves unsure, He is steadfast in performing and perfecting His will in us. He knows what He's doing and He doesn't require our goodness at all. In fact, He is uninterested in our perfectionism or drives to be good, because, compared to His holiness, our good deeds are trashy.

Scripture uses the term "rags". Isaiah 64:6 states, *"All our righteous acts are like filthy rags"* (NIV). On a radio show, I heard a minister say that the prophet's term 'filthy rags' was similar to our understanding of a used sanitary napkin. Yeah—gross. Some of us are on our cycles at this very moment, so we know this is not an appealing paradigm. Of course, we recognize that blood is important and vital to our lives. It's a good thing! We can't live without it. But imagine a doctor offering up a used pad to someone in need of a blood transfusion. That would be insulting and completely disgusting. That's the way our goodness compares to God's holiness. It doesn't fulfill our calling. Our goodness does nothing for the salvation, healing, or perfecting that He alone can produce in our hearts. He sees our so-called "goodness", and it is not up to par. But the profound thing is that He still wants us dearly! Our dirty, dingy rags would never be clean without His holiness and the washing of His glorious love over us. He shed His blood to purify our spiritual, emotional, mental, and physical imperfections. This purity is why we live for Jesus! This purity is why we depend on His goodness and not our own. It's because His loving kindness and goodness are always truthful and always sincere. He never changes, but He desires to change each of us into an image of Christ to reflect His glorious goodness everywhere we go. We won't always understand His ways, but, in faith, we can trust this work as we follow Him on this journey. We can love Him and live for Him in this life and into eternity because He is always good. And our goodness lies in Him.

Wisdom and Folly

One of the things I love so much about being a woman is that we all carry a mystery about us. It takes the heart of a king to discover the ways of a woman. We are intriguing and accomplished; we are tender yet strong. We were blessed with an intellect that sees beyond the mere black and white of a matter. My husband and I don't always see things from the same perspective. I've told him many times in the past, "you draw straight lines with pencils, and I scribble scrabble in pastel colors!"

Women are glorious creatures! We were the last to be created—the culmination of God's creativity. But too many of us are insistent on doing life our way. Sometimes, we can be manipulative and demanding of others. We don't always want to be corrected. We don't want someone telling us we are wrong. This reaction is a result of believing the world's lies that our lives are our business. But we know this is not true. If we are in Christ, we have been purchased with the precious blood from the cross. We don't have the freedom to do whatever we want, how we want, when we want, or with whom we want. The Bible declares: *"You are not your own. For you were bought at a price"* (1 Corinthians 6:19-20 NKJV). It's not our prerogative to direct our lives, and it's foolish to live as if it were. If something does not glorify Jesus, then it's not wise to do it.

Right before I moved to Greensboro and met my husband, I went to visit a girl whom I'd known in college. She was a sweet girl, but often times I tried to avoid her because she was a "real" Christian type. During my partying days, she made me feel guilty. She was so nice and friendly, but I felt embarrassed around her. She was always trying to hug me and tell me she loved me. I'm smiling now because Charity's prayers over me truly reached God's heart. He heard her prayers for me; I am sure of this. She carried herself with so much wisdom. Small in frame, she had a big heart and a confidence that I couldn't understand. Eventually, we became good friends and she sort of mentored me as a sister in Christ.

Once I accepted Jesus, I began spending more time with her. She was aware that I had lost all of my friends. Because I had no one to talk to, I confided in her about some of my struggles during my first few months of salvation. Often she would listen and give me a scripture. Sometimes I'd receive it, but other times I'd get upset because her words were often uncomfortable to hear. But I knew she spoke the truth, and I wanted to be as committed to Christ as she was.

"Trina, that's foolish," she would bluntly say to me. "Is what you're doing worth Christ's blood?" she would ask. That question will never leave me. I plan to ask my daughter this same question once she comes of age and begins to make her own choices. I want to ask you the same: "Is what you're doing worth Christ's blood?" The decisions we make are a direct reflection of the worth we see in the blood Jesus Christ shed to purchase us. In our minds, we are wise, but in our choices we can be foolish if we neglect remembering that Christ's power can keep us from bad decisions. We sometimes excuse away wrong choices to appease a culture that urges us to deny the power of Christ within us. But John 3:20 says, *"For everyone who does evil hates the Light, and does not come to the Light for fear that his deeds will be exposed"* (NASB).

For support, we need to surround ourselves with those who will affirm us in the faith and walk with us as we venture forth, with love and wisdom. We operate in spiritual immaturity when we set ourselves up as our own authorities and live lives void of correction and instruction from others. And according to the Bible, it's foolish to do so. I had Charity, but you have someone else. It's essential to connect with those who will both encourage and correct us. Wisdom loves correction because it produces right living and preserves our hearts (Ecclesiastes 7:12). Folly rejects correction, as a foolish heart feels comfortable in wrongdoing.

Proverbs Chapter 9 contrasts the two:

> *"Wisdom has built her house...she calls from the highest point of the city, "Let all who are simple come to my house!" To those who have no sense she says, "Leave your simple ways and you will live; walk in the way of insight." Whoever corrects a mocker invites insults; whoever rebukes the wicked incurs abuse. Do not rebuke mockers or they will hate you; rebuke the wise and they will love you...The fear of the Lord is the beginning of wisdom, and knowledge of the Holy One is understanding...If you are wise, your wisdom will reward you; if you are a mocker,*

> *you alone will suffer. Folly is an unruly woman; she is simple and knows nothing. She sits at the door of her house...calling out to those who pass by..."Let all who are simple come to my house!" To those who have no sense she says, "Stolen water is sweet; food eaten in secret is delicious! But little do they know that the dead are there, that her guests are deep in the realm of the dead"* (NIV).

I've often wondered why the Bible likens both characters to women. I believe it's because women are influential and persuasive. In our bodies, we have the potential to bring life and change the world. And, so it is in our spiritual lives as well. It's a wise woman who recognizes that she will accomplish good things by aligning her life with God's Word for His glory. A foolish woman lives in hiding. She is vexed toward what is right and true, yet she's open to following others into compromise and wrong living. Folly enjoys the lies that seduce with immediate pleasure. She doesn't realize that she is caught in a trap; she does the same things with different people, expecting better results. She's basic in her mindset and is spiritually unaccomplished. Lacking discernment, she follows the crowd and does whatever they do. She blends in with her surroundings and rejects those who live differently. She's a hypocrite. She has no light. She avoids what is required of her and prefers to do things in secret. After her fun is over, she wonders why she is so lost and empty and then blames others for her misery. Folly is paranoid that she is always being judged because the weight of her guilt has convicted her already. Her sin brings shame upon her. She is easily offended and lashes out at sound advice. She never takes responsibility for herself. She never gives; she only takes. She disregards the lives and feelings of others because she is blinded by her own selfishness. She demands blessings but reaps penalties because she insists on practicing what God says to renounce. She expects to be appreciated for things she has not done and attributes she does not poses. She is shallow and hollow and lost.

Wisdom, on the other hand, can perceive the future and prepares herself for success. She recognizes that she was once foolish, but instead of repeating her failures, she embraces the correction she's received and moves forward in obedience to the instruction given her. She desires God's goodness, and she focuses on pleasing Him. Wisdom rejects the excuses of this world. She understands she is living for more than fake applause and temporary attention. She has no time for things that have no value. She is unmoved by fleeting pleasures that are over within moments. She is intentional about life and devotes herself to what will keep her set apart. She invests in encouraging others and she is open to learning and growing, no matter how uncomfortable it might feel. She sets goals and achieves them. She has aspirations and takes on the responsibility to make her dreams a reality. She doesn't want to look like other women. She doesn't want to be overtaken by the crowds that follow Folly. Wisdom is aware of where Christ is taking her, and she's unwilling to let anyone or anything steal the treasures that God has promised her. She prayers for spiritual increase and her prayers are heard by God. She rejects compromise because she knows it results in folly. She strongly encourages others to join her in her Godly pursuits. She opens her heart and joyfully shares what she has. She isn't spoiled by empty compliments. She is not infatuated with herself. Wisdom is a woman who cares about the lives and souls of others, and she fervently loves those God has placed around her.

Every day we face opportunities and circumstances that call us to make either wise or foolish choices. We can either operate as Folly or as Wisdom. The choice is ours and ours alone. We cannot blame others for the outcomes of our bad decisions, and we should not turn our face when we see those we know and love making wrong choices. In Christ, we are accountable to each other. Galatians 6:1 instructs, *"Brothers and sisters, if someone is caught in a sin, you who live by the Spirit should restore that person gently. But watch yourselves, or you also may be tempted"* (NIV).

Wisdom reaches out and inquires God's direction. She encourages and corrects. She invites others to join her in successful, righteous living, by aligning her living with her words. Wisdom sets standards for herself and others. She doesn't compromise because she is focused on God's goodness. Her mirror is God's Word, and her beauty comes from a heart of love for Christ. Folly rejects and denies righteousness. She parades her compromises publicly but cries in secret over her regrets. She lives a life of denial while evading honesty and obedience. She laughs at the choices of those who desire to please God, and then she complains when she must endure the consequences of her compromise. The two women are at odds with one another: Wisdom reaches out to Folly, but Folly rejects Wisdom. They are of two different spirits and therefore are ultimately headed in two different directions. Each of us has the choice of following after one or the other. Which type of woman do you want to be? You cannot follow both at the same time.

Comparisons, Lists and Lipstick

Beth Moore once said, "I love women! Tall women, old women, young women, single, and married women".

Praise God for women! We are strong and fierce and passionate and explosively innovative! I would never wish to be a man. Thank God for them, but being a woman is something special. Still, we, too, have our shortcomings. As women, we are faced with a certain personal foe every single day of our lives. We are so familiar with this enemy that we are seldom aware that it needs to be combatted. So we go about our days experiencing defeat, largely unaware. We've been so inundated with the attacks and the traps set out for us that we aren't even concerned with our lack of victory in this area. In many ways, this foe has chained us, keeping us so bound up and confined that we are hindered from our growth in the Lord. You'd think that a snare this treacherous would be a great concern, but we aren't concerned. In some cases, we are actually even attracted to it. We want more of it, and we spend money to improve it. We use it to brand ourselves and build imaginary thrones. It is our glory, our idol, and often our excuse to lean on ourselves instead of God. I'm talking about our self-image.

Forget about the celebrities and the magazines that market images to us. We compare ourselves to our co-workers, our sisters, and our friends. We want to be the 'Queen' of the crop! We want to prove our worth and affirm our abilities; not for who we are, but for what we have, what we look like, and where we are trying to go. Womanhood has become the "battle of the sexy". The world keeps trying to re-label us as "females"—belittling our gloriously God-ordained identities. Emphasis lies on what we can get, how we can get it, and from whom we can get it. But in God's kingdom, this will not do. To gain our lives, we must be willing to lose them, Luke 17:33 says. But no one is teaching this to us anymore. No one is telling us our value has nothing to do with our image. We are beautiful, and we should celebrate that. We should delight in our different gifts and rock that red lipstick! But, when it's all said and done, our hearts and spirits shouldn't be neglected at the expense of our outward temples. Our bodies ought not be our gods. Petty things pass away. Too many of us are more consumed with what will one day wrinkle and age. Confusion over what defines beauty steals our capacity to display the true beauty of Christ. "Why should we resolve to be like Christ", we ponder. People like us better this way. We throw shade because it's funny. We binge on TV that makes us feel like the way we are living is appropriate for this day and age. We show skin hoping to snag attention and fame in our own right. We teeter with limits in our relationships and grow greedy in our consumption. But deep inside, we are churning with dissatisfaction. So we go to church looking for an outlet where we can wash away the regrets of yesterday only to leave the pew and walk back into a culture that ensnares us. Where is our victory? Where is our resolve? My friends, I promise you, it's not in self-help, self-improvement or self-determination. It's not in the mirror, in our closets or bank accounts. It's only in Jesus.

I'm reminded of the woman in the Bible who lost a coin. Jesus tells this parable in the Gospel of Luke. She has ten coins, yet loses one. She abandons the other nine as she frantically searches to find the missing one. Jesus likens this to how we should search for the kingdom of Heaven and how He, the King of Heaven, chooses to search for us. But there is another lesson in this story that I find so profound. The woman was so insistent on finding what would make her whole that she was willing to lose herself to attain it. She didn't put off her search for another day. She didn't compromise by finding temporary satisfaction in the remaining nine she had. She didn't excuse herself with the lie that, "this is good enough for now." No. Scripture says that this woman sought the missing coin with all of her might, and once she found it, she called all of her friends to join her in celebration. She resolved to do what needed to be done to get what would make a difference in her life (Luke 15:8-10).

Ladies, are we so determined to be made whole that we are willing to abandon everything that makes sense in our culture in the process of attaining Christ, even if it means sacrificing self-images? Do we understand that our value, our self-worth, and our identity can only be found through a relationship with God—the very One who created within us our longing to be cherished and seen?

There was a time in my life where I didn't understand such things. I depended on my long legs, my vanity, my intellect, and my social connections to make me feel approved. I thought my value was in how many friends I had and how many parties I attended. I stacked up my contracts and built my portfolio. I tried to find meaning in my paychecks. I believed the lie that I could never be acceptable by God because I couldn't get things right. It felt impossible on my own, so I concluded that I wasn't strong enough. I so intensely believed this lie and struggled to find meaning and beauty every day. I piled on more and more judgment on myself, all the while seeming to enjoy life. Inside though, I was tired. My attempts to find worth in my life through my own actions and in my own ways left me bare. I couldn't find a sense of my "goodness" anywhere. All I was really doing was comparing myself with others—my classmates, my model mates, my cousins, and my roommates. When they seemed to excel, it intimidated me; when they seemed to fail, it convinced me that I wasn't so bad off. We've all competed and compared. It doesn't make our lives better. It just makes our existence pitiful.

When I use to go on model calls and auditions—a "go-see" in model's terms—I'd always scan the room as I waited for my name to be called. Now, I think I'm cute, but when you are in a room with thirty other gorgeous faces, who all look similar to you, well, it's easy for the comparison laser beams to start shooting off. I don't care how confident you are, when there is only one open space and thirty-five people that you are up against, it makes for a very nervous experience. I learned quickly, that it's best to be as early as possible to any audition in order to avoid the quiet gazes from dozens of blue, brown, and green eyes seizing you as you enter a room. I'm guilty of doing the same, unfortunately. Contrary to popular belief, models are nice girls for the most part. We exchange smiles, and we hug familiar people we've worked with on previous jobs. It's easy to make a friend for the day. But there's no doubt about it: at most auditions, you sit in a room for thirty minutes where you are quietly comparing and being compared by others. If an audition was for girls at a particular height, I always seemed to be the shortest girl in the room, even though I'm five feet ten inches! If the call was for a girl aged twenty with curly hair, there'd be at least five other girls in the room with prettier and bouncier curls than mine. In would come self-doubt and inaccurate assessments.

Comparisons are toxic. It's easy to notice what we don't have when we see others with more, but by measuring ourselves against other women, we fail to appreciate what we do have. This is true spiritually as well. Sometimes, we even compare ourselves with others who seem to be excelling in ministry. Spiritual comparisons with other believers cause us to judge ourselves inwardly. We then make projections outwardly through lenses of intimidation. We become performance-oriented and make lists of "do's" and "don'ts." We place ourselves in a religious hierarchy that has no place in God's kingdom. These lists foster self-righteousness and leave God out. They bring out cattiness and pettiness, and they prey on our insecurities. We become judgmental and critical. Lists cause us to look to our own efforts, our own power, and our own strengths (or self-proclaimed strengths). I carried many spiritual comparison lists in my heart as a young Christian, and they suffocated me. Aren't your checklists doing the same?

We carry lists to prove to ourselves and to others that we are better, stronger, and more capable than others. But it's only a fading façade—like red lipstick that's been dabbed on a napkin. The changes we make and the lifestyle we live for Christ should be based on our relationship with Him. Physical attainment doesn't prove our worth. Spiritual attainment isn't evidence that we are more loved by God. We have nothing to prove. In truth, we all need Christ who lives within, and a list isn't going to solve that need. Stop looking at your list. In fact, just stop making lists altogether. Who cares that you have never had a drink in your whole life? Who cares that at least you're not having sex? Who cares that you don't swear as much as you used to or that you don't smoke weed anymore? You're still a sinner. Your list doesn't make you closer to God than the person who can't check any of those things off. The fact that we keep lists is proof that we need saving. We only make lists for things that we need help with and as reminders to ourselves that we have to do better, but lists won't make us any better. They only show our lack and great need for the Lord.

Too often, instead of bringing our lists to the One who can fulfill every need, we whip them out in readiness to compare. We puff ourselves up, justifying our flaws and unknowingly belittling others in the process. This tendency to compare can become an obsession; it's what we do to keep our self-perceptions intact, to prove our goodness to ourselves. But pride is the root. Scripture says: *"However, when they measure themselves with themselves and compare themselves with one another, they are without understanding and behave unwisely"* (2 Corinthians 10:12 NLT). Comparison does not make for the abundant life in Christ. Grace is not found in making lists. It's time to rip them up, humble our selves and receive God's help to perfect our insufficiencies. We have not been called to perfect ourselves. No matter how much we try and strive and "fake it 'til we make it," there is no self-help for the soul. "Self" has no power or authority when it comes to spiritual transformation. We cannot fix our hearts. If we could, then God would not have had to send Jesus.

Once I realized that I am already complete in Christ, I began to notice my lenses changing toward others. I wasn't so quick to notice petty things like someone's shoes or hair or the clothes they wore. I became less obsessed with superficial things and more intrigued by the hearts and personalities of the people I came across. I began to see the power I have to be an encourager and a motivator. As I've stated before, God has blessed women to be life-givers. This gifting is not just in the physical, but also in the spiritual, emotional, and relational. What you produce can and most definitely will change the world. You, my sister, have the God-given ability to produce life wherever you go! Comparisons destroy our life-giving abilities. And competition aborts our relationships with the ones called to create life with us. But we don't have to live this way. We have the power, through Christ, to be content with who He is creating us to be! 1 Corinthians 7:17 provides wisdom: *"Let each person lead the life that the Lord has assigned to him, and to which God has called him"* (ESV).

Competition has no place in God's kingdom! Your life is especially and specifically for you to live. There are too many blessings for you to enjoy, too many ministries for you to serve in, too much impact that only you can make, and too many lessons that are meant only for you to learn. You don't have time to look into someone else's life and compare yours with theirs. I don't have time to analyze your calling when God needs my full attention concerning mine. Let's stay focused on Christ's example and not on ourselves so much! Let Christ who lives within your heart flow out. Create life in the relationships you are connected to. Speak life-giving words from the Word over your worries, your limitations, and your future as you journey with Jesus! Celebrate the successes that God is blessing others with, knowing that in time, He will bless you as well, if you'll stay focused on obeying Him.

I hope we will always be women who seek out opportunities to inspire souls for Christ; doing this can be so difficult in today's society where shade is popular and mean girls are admired. But these characteristics have no place in hearts consumed with loving Jesus. Because of Christ, we are different. We live differently, and we behave differently. God is calling us to be not only peculiar people, but also peculiar women (see 1 Peter 2:9). We're to be humble in our hearts, confident in our faith, competitive only with ourselves, and eager to lavish our love on all we come in contact with, whether they appreciate it or not. You are equipped and blessed to be victorious as you accomplish all that Christ has purposed in your life! Don't let the doubt of the enemy steal the power of life that God has graced for you to create and share! Competition has no place in the heart of a child of God. We are all beautiful and dearly loved with much to gain and much to share.

#BeTheShe

Having a clear view of God's great love will lead you to a proper view of yourself. Until we understand that only valuable things have real purpose, we will spend our lives chasing shadows: aimlessly searching for what does not exist. Your time and your heart are too precious to waste. Scripture likens a wasted life to treasure that gets eaten by moths or wealth that is eventually corrupted by rust (see

Matthew 6:19-20). When we set our eyes on what our own abilities can achieve, we treasure corruptible things. Our value does not lie within ourselves or in our attachments. We are valuable because God says we are. We are valuable because He created us in His image, through His creative imagination and by the power of His word. It's time we embrace this reality and give it more than just acknowledgment.

When we begin to embrace the truths that we are women whose hearts are set in Heavenly places with Christ—women with an existence unfolding in front of angelic beings, whose decisions impact eternity—we find that our choices begin to be motivated differently. We discover, as well, that our motives and attitudes aren't so self-centered. The results accomplish meaning and purpose, which radiate from the smallest choices we face.

Being a Christian doesn't make us perfect, but we are being perfected! As the Lord unveils His will for us, we'll begin to discover joy and purpose and freedom! In our victories, we are encouraged. In our weaknesses, God gives us His strength! It doesn't matter what anyone else insists. It doesn't matter if no one understands. Know who you are in Christ. We are all apart of God's kingdom, if we have accepted the gift of salvation. Lay aside those things that will hinder and distract you from running the race of the Christian life. Our concerns must consist of more than our hair, our nails and the next weekend. People are watching you. Our world is looking for women like you to love well, lead well, and build legacies. We must be sensitive to the lives surrounding ours. Let's be their examples in the faith—their models for Christ. There will be times when you are misunderstood. Sometimes your confidence will be perceived as haughtiness. But you don't have to succumb to the petty perspectives of others. Live your life with the confidence of Christ and as valued women on mission to impact hearts and minds for God's kingdom. Let your love speak in place of your words and embrace every moment of transformation that Christ is developing within you.

Our Heavenly Father is quite satisfied with the plans He has in store. Each of us has a different role, and each of us are necessary parts of the Body of Christ. All that's inside us is there on purpose: the beautiful, the hormonal, the passive and aggressive, the innocence and maturity. If you are social, it's because you are supposed to be. If you are shy, this personality trait is not a mistake. If you have a temper, celebrate the fact that you have passion. However, allow the Holy Spirit to teach you self-control. If you are always looking on the bright side, thank God that you harbor hope; but allow the Holy Spirit to give you discernment. Unapologetically live each day with passion and confidence of your calling. Be the "she" that Christ has appointed you to be! You don't need to be anyone else, and you don't need to be afraid of what lies dormant within you. Whoever "she" is, "she" is radiant and beautiful in Christ. And it's time to give her permission to exist!

#BeTheShe is an anthem I have come to live by—a reminder that in Christ, I can be anything in every situation. I do not lack in Christ, so when I need to be courageous, I can access courage in Him! When I need to be a peacemaker, Jesus will provide the wisdom required. Christ is our source in all things, and from His heart, we can access all that we need to live in abundance and to become the women we're destined to be. In our social media/hash tag world, women are commodities, but in God's kingdom, we are matchless. We are each a force to be reckoned with! Our very existence causes intimidation within the spiritual realm by our ferocious feminine disposition to love, to worship and to build community. This is kingdom work.

I think a woman's heart is astonishing. Out of the same heart comes both timidity and powerful gumption! God knows our hearts very well. He knows them because He shaped them for Himself. We can fill our lives up with people and things, but they won't provide the sustenance for which our hearts cry. These things don't fit. We already know that. But sometimes we still try! Why do we still try? We should all know by now, nothing outside of Christ can ever be the anchor for our souls.

You have a beauty and a power that exceeds any form of goodness this world wants to offer you. It's imperative that you understand your value, so you can discover your full purpose. Honey, you were born to soar. As my friend Ashley so eloquently quotes her mother, "We aren't chickens clucking around for handouts. We are eagles and we soar!" Do you sense that you are soaring in your current life? If not, you should be. You are the only one who is limiting you. In John 14:12, Jesus tells us that we can do even greater works than He did. Thus in Jesus' name, there is nothing that you can't do or become. But you definitely won't do anything if you choose to do nothing. Don't waste your life.

You, my sister, are powerful. You, my sister, are valuable. People don't waste things that are cherished. I'm not going to order dinner at Ruth's Chris and then take my plate and dump it on the floor. I'm not going to shred my paycheck for *any* reason! Never should we dump or shred our lives; we must understand our value in God's eyes! That's why, as Christian women, we don't give ourselves away to men for entertainment. We are too valuable. We don't expose our flesh and flaunt our womanly parts to attract social media attention because we know we are sacred. We don't waste our time by advertising or inviting temporary attention from people who don't value us. We have been called to be set apart! We have believed our Heavenly Father who says we're cherished and loved! Dirty words have no place in our mouths. Instead, we use conversations only to build others up and never to tear them down (Ephesians 4:29). We do this because we recognize the value God has placed on all people. This life we live is not our own! The kingdom God has bestowed on us is beyond this world. We are the diamonds and pearls of Heaven—the crowned jewels of Christ. We are daughters of the King, and we are homesick for our thrones!

So we must bring Heaven down. We must call upon the power of the Holy Spirit and seek our God with wholeheartedness so that we can share the goodness of His gospel wherever we go. This pursuit is our greatest calling and highest priority, but requires that we first develop an understanding of who we are in Him. Let's not waste our time on trivial things or vanities. There is no longer room for competition, bickering, or compromise once we understand the value God's placed on our lives and the purpose He has for us individually and collectively. There are too many hearts and souls that need to be reached by those of us who operate in the love of Christ. The Lord has called us to broadcast the truth of salvation within our world. We are to radiate Him. How can this work be accomplished if we insist on depending on ourselves rather than His goodness? Our value is never about what we can do, it's always about what He is doing in us.

Listen, through salvation, you have the Savior of the world residing within your hearts and, if you are not quite there yet in developing your relationship with Christ, it's never too late. If you truly desire to have Him awaken your heart and give you Heavenly horizons, ask the Lord to do so. We must believe He is able if we are to become women of God's design. Do you see your salvation and relationship with Jesus as valuable? With our mouths we say "yes," but what do we do with our choices? My sisters, I promise you, whatever it is that you are battling with or trying to fit in with your Christianity, it won't work. It has no eternal value and therefore no purpose in the context of the future that God wants to bring forth for you. My prayer is that we decide, here and now to be the "she" who is unashamed of the Gospel. We must cooperate with Christ to become the masterpiece that He desires to create. Money won't make you whole. Parties won't eliminate your loneliness. Relationships won't give you meaning. Those friends you bend over backward for...is it worth losing your very self? That man who keeps trying to push the limits, is it worth your self-respect and dignity? His false promises will only lead to further empty claims. And that's not love. Your value far surpasses being chased or charmed.

And let me stop here, please. There is a difference between being pursued and being chased. I don't think many of us know the difference. I once had a conversation with a girl who told me that all it takes is a compliment and she is sold. First off, your heart is not a tool to be bought and sold. Second, let's not be so easily impressed or so thirsty for affection. You can complement yourself! You don't need anybody to tell you that you're pretty. Look in the mirror and tell yourself you are gorgeous! That's what I do! It's not vanity to celebrate the truth. Believe your own affirmations, and maintain standards for those to whom you give your heart. Your love is valuable; your heart is to be pursued and not chased.

Think about the animal kingdom. In that kingdom are lions and hyenas. A hyena chases and kills other animals but not always because it's hungry. Sometimes, they just like to hunt and kill things. It's a thrill for them. Once they've gotten their prey, they move on to chase and kill the next animal. Eventually, they will kill to eat, but they discard countless carcasses in their path. Hyenas create destruction and drama. They have no care or concern beyond their instinctive drive to conquer something.

Then there is the lion. A lion will keenly study its target. Sometimes for days, this animal will endure hunger as it waits for the perfect choice. Once it has made its decision, the lion tracks down the animal it hunts and pursues it single-mindedly. Once he has possession of the target, he consumes it; he wastes nothing. The lion is strategic. It doesn't go after random things. Lions are specific in what they pursue.

A man who expects the devotion of your physical love, outside of a marriage commitment, is a hyena. He is only interested in the chase and odds are, once he has hunted you down, he will discard you. Raise your hand if you know what I mean! Ladies, we are worthy of lions! You are worthy of a man who will take his time in pursuing you. You can be the "she" who waits for a man who will study you and "consume" you into himself so that the two of you become one being in the covenant of marriage. Any man who offers less is not worthy of your time. Use wisdom. Stop compromising your hearts for boys who are only interested in a momentary game of chase. Know who you are and whose you are! Don't settle for less. A man of God is what we all long for—someone kind and loving, committed to Christ and passionate for us. We want someone we can trust with our children, someone who knows how to get in touch with God and knows how to lead well. These traits come from Christ, and this is the kind of man God wants to give you as His blessing. You don't have to settle. Your value surpasses a chase.

OK...sorry...where were we? Oh yeah....

This world has done an absolute disservice to us regarding our identity and value. All the lies oppose us like headlights; and if we are not planted carefully in the Word, we could become blind to the truths that proclaim we are to live above the standards of this world. We're to live in purity until marriage, love our enemies, wait patiently for God's timing, consider the feelings of others before our own, and pray without ceasing. Everything God calls us to do, Christ has already done. Jesus is waiting until HIS marriage. He chose to love HIS enemies. Even now, HE is waiting patiently for God's timing before He returns. He allowed HIMSELF to die because He chose to think of us first.

We can't become the women God has called us to be outside of valuing what He values; and what He values is you! In our day to day, we can choose to #BeTheShe who loves, who grinds, who hopes and who prays. God's Holy Spirit has equipped us and continues to equip us with each experience we endure and every self-discovery we encounter. We have so much to offer and so much to give. We are delicate and dangerous. We are beautiful and brave. We are purposed with destiny for spiritual accomplishments in this life that will continue to reverberate into the next.

I don't know about you, but I desire to walk in my calling though it may cost me my comfort. Nothing of value is free. Our salvation wasn't free for God. Jesus paid a great price to restore our souls. He sees your value because He is the one who has implanted Him-self in you. He asks that you allow Him to cultivate the life of Christ within you. Is it always easy? No. But those of us who are seeking God are not seeking easy. We are seeking eternity! Know who you are and be willing to trust God in His process of perfecting you. Learn to #BeTheShe who embraces the great purposes and promises of God. Once you finally accept the truth of your value in Him, the thought of settling for anything less becomes insulting.

Standards to Stand On

I once had a girl look across the table at me and accuse me of being judgmental. "Judgy" was the word she used. I was in the middle of making a comment about a situation she had shared by trying to use scripture and showing her a different perspective. Her reaction devastated me. I was so troubled that encouraging her to make Christ-centered decisions was so upsetting to her. From her perspective, to be friends meant my going along with what she wanted to do, so the moment I suggested, "I don't think that's God's best for you," was the moment I became her opponent. The potential friendship I thought was blooming, quickly turned into a war zone and I continue to pray for healing with this particular member of my extended family.

The world shouts from the streets, "tolerance, tolerance!", but blocks anything contrary to its own agenda. Our friends at work are friendly until we take a stand. Our family members love to include us, until we refuse to participate in gossip...so what is a Christian girl to do? Many of us cower in fear of being labeled "judgmental." It's the ultimate insult in our social circles. But if we desire to be authentic Christians, we must accept the fact that our standards set us apart and often offend onlookers who aren't living for Christ. Relationships are all about loving and loving authentically. We must be willing to speak and live out the truth, in love; not to condemn, but to guide others into a harmonious relationship with God. These standards will sometimes separate us from those we love, but their offense is not with you. Not really. They may perceive that you think you are superior, but this is not your doing or your intentions. They just don't recognize God inside you because they can't relate to what they don't have.

For others' sakes, it's so important to maintain the standards that God has set before us. People are watching you the moment you profess Christ. They will dissect and analyze you, and yes, sometimes even envy you. It's a powerful position we have—the position of bearing the name of Jesus. The world identifies Him with you, and some are yearning to discover if He's real. So, the way we socialize, how we converse, the way we dress and even the manner in which we date and love our husbands are all essential to our testimony and our reflection of Jesus.

Adopting the world's passive perspective on kingdom issues is a detriment to our relationship with Christ and the influence we've been called to have. I've always found it odd that promiscuity has become permissible in the hearts of "God-fearing" women who are seeking marriage. And I'm not just talking about the act of sexual intercourse, although the percentage of Christian women who maintain abstinence until marriage is below 44%.* I'm talking more specifically about the mentality of promiscuity: the decision buried deep within our hearts to cut corners in our relationships and disregard the Bible's clear standards of purity. Purity includes not only how we handle our bodies but also how we dress them, how we interact with the opposite sex, and even how we portray ourselves to others. The girls who wear the least amount of clothes get the highest number of "likes" on social media, and it saddens me that some of us who claim Christ under our statuses deny Him with our photos. We allow the world to carry us away with their morals, or lack thereof, instead of standing firm on the decrees of God in scripture. There are so many broken hearts who have fallen prey to the deception that high standards make for a boring life or that cutting corners will secure a relationship or fame. Listen,

---

* Jamie Calloway-Hanauer, "The Age of Abstinence—Only Sex Ed is Over," *Christianity Today,* July 2013, accessed March 1, 2015, http://www.christianity-today.com/women/2013/july/age-of-abstinence-only-sex-ed-is-over.html.

you have been called to be more than just a girlfriend. Your beauty far exceeds the amount of "likes" you can get on social media. The truth again is in the Word: *"The backslider gets bored with himself; the Godly man's life is exciting"* (Proverbs 14:14 TLB). So often, we learn our lessons only in the regrets.

On our second date, my husband told me he wanted to marry me. I thought he was crazy, but he was quite serious. A few months later, he said he wanted to buy a house so that I wouldn't have to come home to an apartment once we were married. He bought a house the week before my twenty-sixth birthday. Although his college life was that of chaos, he was proud of his one year of celibacy and often shared with me how he knew it was only by God's power. We were so young and could have so easily done what was expected of a young couple in love to do, but though it was difficult and though we both received our fair share of teasing, we were determined to please Christ. At no point did we ever break up in our three-year dating relationship. He was forward, and I was shy…at first. We spent afternoons with friends, enjoyed live bands under the stars, and sought Godly counsel. We kept Christ involved in our dating, even when it would have been easier not to. We kept ourselves accountable to others. We set standards, and we didn't deviate from them. When we were out of line, we very quickly got back in line. We weren't perfect, but we were determined.

I was twenty-eight years old when I married Jarrett McCain. Throughout our entire relationship, the central theme of our love was waiting until marriage. Now, I know that might seem far out there for many of us, but I promise you, we aren't the only ones. We had some afternoons where we needed to reevaluate ourselves, and we certainly found reasons to extend our evening curfews, but our standards remained the same. We upheld purity until marriage by the grace of

God, who taught us how to operate in His standards. When I walked down the aisle on June 1, 2013, I held my head up high in my white dress! I had no shame and nothing to hide. We said our vows with confidence and excitement and we were unashamed before God.

The sacrifices we made to set high standards during dating are still producing blessings in our marriage now. You see, our standards produced favor because favor follows obedience and blessings follow sacrifice. People ask me all the time, "What is your relationship with Jarrett like?" My answer is that our love is secure. He treasures me and not just from moment to moment, but into our future. He often says, "I loved you before I knew you". I am blessed—Forever Blessed—to have such a man of standard, but I didn't receive him by compromising. My desire was to please Christ first, because I had come to know who I am in Him. I'm not always confident, but I am consistent. None of us will ever be perfect, but obedience produces a platform for Christ's perfection, in every area—not just in dating. His standards elevate those who choose to stand upon them. A light on the floor won't shed as much light as one that is placed on the table. You and I can't expect to be women of impact if our standards aren't set in Heavenly places. Keep them up, because they separate the temporary from the eternal.

I'm including this section because there are too many ministries out there, too many teachings, too many books that aren't focusing on the truth of the matter when it comes to purity and sexuality and the setting of standards in various other areas we face. It's not about willpower. None of us have that. Sex is spiritual, but it is also very, very physical. We've all heard the argument, "sex is natural", and so it is; which is why it's such a difficult temptation to combat in our own strength. Our natural drive fights against maintaining the spiritual standards we know we ought to keep. We each have struggled with purity in some form or another. In the modeling industry, I have waged war with myself about my image. Sexually provocative poses open more doors than images for department store catalogs. And more than once, I have been faced with the decision and pressure to keep my clothes on or take them off, in the presence of male strangers. I'm serious.

Our choices boil down to standards. For whom are you living? Who is your Lord? Who are you choosing to represent in this world? Ask yourself how you view your very existence, your femininity, and the state of your spiritual life. The perspectives you harbor about yourself are a reflection on how you view your relationship with God. He declares that we have been made in His image (Genesis 1:27). Therefore, we take care of our-selves and respect the hearts of others, because God values us all. We don't deceive or use people to get what we want. We don't manipulate our husbands to finagle our desired outcomes. We don't catch attitudes with people or pressure them into cooperating with us. We don't string men along —pretending to be romantically interested in them when we really aren't. This might be acceptable in our culture, but it is deplorable behavior for someone who desires to please the Lord. How can we honestly say we love God, yet mistreat people who have been made in His image (1 John 4:20)? People perceive the truth of who you are by your care, or lack of care, for others. Your portrayal of yourself through the standards you set answer these questions far more than your words ever will.

To the Single and Married Ones

Andrea, my sister-in-law, has been a warm, glowing light in my life. She is constantly building others up and nudging them into the glory of God's love. She's served as president of one of the top college sororities on her campus and now finds professional achievement in her career and in her personal serving ministry. She is successful in every sense of the word, and she is a "good girl" if there ever was one. But even she insists on the need to set standards for herself through God's eyes and not her own.

She told me once, "Before Ben and I got married, we set standards and committed our relationship to prayer. I prayed that God would confirm to my heart His will for the marriage because I wanted His best for me. I loved Ben, but I didn't want to walk into any future that might have been out of line for my life. I wanted God's will no matter how much I thought I was in love." What an incredible example!

There will always be the great possibility that God's standards will block us from what we think we want, but God's provision is always better! Don't think of it as a prohibition, but think of it as a safeguard.

To all the single ladies: being labeled 'stuck up" or "judgmental" because of your standards is a scary thing, but you should never apologize for living Biblical principles. They are cloaks of protection! Drama occurs when we fail to set standards. A woman who cannot turn down a date is a woman with low self-esteem. Our ability to be selective is based entirely on our self-worth. And our self-worth is connected to our ability to set standards. I know the dating "game" can be an unnerving one. Believe me; I know. But realize that the God who holds your future is able and capable of aligning your life to cross paths with whomever He desires for you. I'm not saying don't be opened to meeting new people. You most definitely should. But I am saying to use wisdom in how and whom you spend your time and your life with. It makes no sense to make bad choices in relationships and then blame and bash the other person for it. Learn to live responsibly and own up to your decisions. Immaturity says to spite someone else for outcomes that don't end favorably for us. This is not effective living. We cannot make the mistake in believing that unwise choices will result in abundance. Live your life on God's standards in your dating. Hold yourself and others accountable for the trajectory of your relationships. When a man is consistent in how he treats you, either positively or negatively, use discernment regarding the appropriate steps to take when moving forward. Remember, habits repeat themselves; a man's good patterns will repeat just as well as his bad ones. The same is true for you. No need to try and "make" him change. He will do so on his own, if he feels compelled to do so. But in the meantime, what will you choose to do? You must make a choice, and such choices should be made based off of your standards. By taking responsibility, rather than blaming or bashing, you find that you will thrive more in your personal life. Not everyone will live up to their promises and not every relationship will lead to marriage. Know your worth and choose wisely. Invoke standards when deciding who you are willing to date, because their lives will most definitely make an impact on yours, and vice versa.

In 2 Corinthians 4:7, Christ calls us *"earthen vessels with treasures,"* but so often we seek to be treasured by other things, though they devalue us. That is not God's best for you. Standards are essential.

The same is true if you're married. Standards shouldn't fall after you've exchanged vows. If you are a Kingdom woman, then you must operate in Kingdom ways. Our husbands are our gifts, not our benefactors; we are to love them and respect them for the position that Christ has bestowed upon them. Remember, marriage is a ministry. It takes devotion, dedication and selflessness to produce love and legacy. Romance is impulsive and circumstantial, but Agape love (love that is eternal and unconditional) is cultivated through intentional fortitude.

Between 2011-2014, my husband and I celebrated five weddings, including our own. Only two of those marriages are still in existence today. According to the American Psychological Association, fifty percent of marriages in the United States end in divorce* and the percentage for failed marriages in the evangelical community is twenty-six percent.† The craze to date, fall in love, and get married won't result in a happy ending without standards. If you want the best from your husband, you must offer the best of yourself just as God offered the best of Himself, through Christ. Your husband, like you, is made in the image of God. Still serve him dinner when you're angry. Kiss him when you're tired. Respect your husband, even if you don't agree with him. Listen, the Holy Spirit often reveals His truth to women first. An example is when the angel told Mary about Christ before Joseph (Matthew 1:18-25; Luke 1:26) and the confirmation of the Lord's resurrection to the women before the other disciples (see Matthew 28:1). It's common for women to possess vaster insights than a man, but if you feel that God has revealed something to you that your husband is not yet aware of, cover him in prayer and wait on the Lord. Odds are, your revelation precedes the appropriate timing. As you pray for your husband, he will be built up in preparation for when God reveals the revelation to him in the suitable time. So, honor your husband as your spiritual leader and submit to him in love, by trusting God to have control…not you.

Our feminist culture tells us we're to be respected before we should give respect, but this is not God's standard. We may feel as if we know better in a situation, and that may be so, but we are to pray

---

* "Marriage and Divorce," *American Psychological Association, http://www.apa.org/topics/divorce.*

† "New Marriage and Divorce Statistics Released," *Barna, https://www.barna.com/research/new-marriage-and-divorce-statistics-released/.*

and not brag. Our responsibility is to commit our revelations to prayer and allow God to plant seeds in our husbands as He prepares their hearts to receive such truths in His appointed time. A woman devoted to prayer lifts her husband up before God. It's not our place to argue, manipulate, or tear down our men for any reason. God's standards require us to respect our husbands and entrust their hearts, minds, and souls to God. In so doing, you'll cultivate a marriage of excellence. I promise, you'll start to see a change in the way you love and in the way you are being loved.

The standard must always be Christ first—in our dating life, marriage, social settings, clothes, business and conversations. We must learn to live by the standards we've set and learn to be without. Waiting is not a bad word. Romantic relationships are not the pinnacle of human existence. And dating doesn't always guarantee marriage. Marriage is a ministry, and if we are honest, not everyone is called to marriage. So whether we are married or single, we must set our hearts on God's standards because we desire God's will. We have been called to display God's greatness and to be set apart into a life that produces His light in the darkness. 1 Peter 2:9 states, "*For you are a chosen people. You are royal priests, a holy nation, God's very own possession. As a result, you can show others the goodness of God, for He called you out of the darkness into His wonderful light*" (NLT).

For those of you who are waiting, I know your struggle all too well. But I encourage you to not deviate from the Bible's teachings. Stand firm on them, because they will raise you up and align you with your destiny. As C.S. Lewis stated, "I am sure that God keeps no one waiting unless He sees that it is good for him to wait."

Learn to be patient and selective. Operate in the confidence of Christ, and don't be so thirsty for results now. Our culture uses sexualized labels to measure a female's value, but that is not the totality of who we are in Christ. Those titles do not depict the fullness of our identity or purpose. Many successes can only be attained during single years. Yet there are those of us who are wasting valuable time as we run after one potential relationship to the next. We need to wait on God while investing our time for His kingdom. A couple compliments and dinner are not worth the flood of regrets that follow bad decisions. You don't need to lower yourself just to hear someone tell you you're beautiful. Christ is in you, so beauty comes automatically.

When my cousin Jasmine met her husband, she was serving on the praise team at their church. They met each other through an eavesdropping conversation she was having with her ex-boyfriend about his baby mama drama. When she hung up the phone, Montel made the comment, "That's not God." I'm laughing because I remember her calling me that night and fussing about this boy in the choir who was all in her business. Four years later they were married. As she developed a heart of praise, she discovered that she had to ditch the drama and raise her standards according to the will and Word of God. In so doing, she made room for more meaningful experiences and relationships in replace of those with no real value.

At her wedding, they announced that their first kiss took place following their vows. Wow! Talk about purity and high standards. Through their relationship with God, Jasmine and Montel proved to the world how beautiful purity truly is. They are a beam of light for so many others, and their example proves the keeping power of Christ. Jazzie, my cousin whom I love, wisely chose to operate in higher standards for herself. And the example she set for me by making a radical change of scenery in her social life, coupled with the resolve she began to practice in her daily decisions and the faith that began to pour from her heart, inspired me beyond understanding.

Marriage and dating aren't the only areas where standards are necessary. The call is to reflect Christ in the totality of our living. We can't live messy lives and do messy things and expect to reap a harvest of favor. There are some situations and relationships we've let ourselves endure which should never have happened in the first place. Although God will bring to pass His will, certain decisions can prolong our arrival at the place God has destined for us. Take the children of Israel for example. Because of their erring ways, what should have been an eleven-day trip to the promised land took them forty years. They endured many unnecessary circumstances because their standards weren't set on God. Their waywardness exposed them to countless hindrances and disappointments (Numbers Chapters 15-25). When we make ourselves available to anything and everything, we should not be surprised when anything or everything shows up.

Living in obedience is the steppingstones to destiny in Christ. We want success in our lives, but are we dedicated in cultivating success in our hearts? We want Godly men, but are we living the Godly lives that will attract a Godly man? Are we standing on the Word's standards or just fancy stilettos? We have expectations on how we should be romanced and treated, but please realize that a Godly man has standards and expectations, too.

Everyone wants Boaz, but not everybody is willing to be Ruth. She had standards, and she lived by them unapologetically. She chose to be obedient in an unfaithful nation where she resolved in her heart to honor God. Ruth was busy working for others; she spent her time helping those in need. She sought the Lord and He led her feet to success for her household as well as an encounter with Boaz. Boaz didn't notice her hips and curves or her nails on fleek. He noticed her heart and her service. He was attracted to her spirit. She didn't have to advertise because her spirit spoke volumes about who she was. She was a woman of God, a woman of high esteem and confidence who didn't have to brag about herself. Her love for God exuded out of her as it does from any woman whose heart is on fire for the Lord (see the book of Ruth in the Old Testament).

I know that in our souls we ache and long for relationships and love. We want our careers to be successful and we want our dreams to come true. But sister, you already have success! A man is not synonymous with your identity. A career is not the fulfillment of your purpose. Each is an addition to a higher calling that is already over your life. Christ is the fulfillment of all we desire. Love Him first and trust the standards He's set in place. Until you become intimate with Christ, you won't have enough vision to recognize a man of God and you won't have the spiritual discernment to navigate your life or career.

Ruth's life is recorded in scripture to forever commemorate her hard work, her faithfulness and her marriage. The blessings she incurred didn't end with her story. Because of her faithfulness, God chose her family bloodline to be that of His Son Jesus Christ! Her Godly standards produced a blossom for eternity—the Lord Himself. The same can be said of you. Like Ruth, you have the freedom to sow seeds of favor or seeds that bring penalty. The results of your standards will affect the futures of the many who are connected to you. Whether you are married or single, keep standards that will lead you and others into a blessed destiny.

Questions for Discussion

1. We live in a time when women are encouraged to oppose each other, compete, and tear one another down. In every reality TV show, we see these behaviors displayed. We see the TV echoed in the dorm room, on social media and sometimes beneath the surface in our own hearts. Rivalry is not just based on physical appearance. If we are honest, sometimes we even compare our ministries with those of others. Why do you think the culture celebrates drama and disharmony between women? As believers, what should our attitude be toward the culture that says throw shade, bash other women, and compete to get ahead?

2. Reflect on the Scriptures below, and record them in the space provided.

   1 Corinthians 1:10

   Colossians 3: 13-14

   1 Peter 3:8

3. In the section *#BeTheShe* , you've read, "Having a clear view of God's great love will lead you to a proper view of yourself." Reflect on this statement. What does this mean to you? And how can you apply it to your own understanding of identity and purpose in Jesus? What type of "She" do you want to be?

PART TWO

TRANSFORMATIONS

CHAPTER 7

From Fear to Faith

Many people walk away from Jesus because of fear—fear that Christian living is too hard, fear of missing out, fear of not being in control anymore, or fear of change. To some degree, we each struggle with fear, but it is our faith that overcomes any natural tendency to distrust God.

Scripture is full of promises from God to guide, comfort and strengthen our souls in the midst of our fears. God's Word tells us that there is hope, and we know that He has no lie within Him (Numbers 23:19). He is the sustainer of every one of us and His goodness is revealed when we find ourselves faced against fearful circumstances. His is our strength and desires to produce great faith in us. Although God is not the giver of fear, our fears can help showcase areas where we need Him most. We combat fears with faith as we allow Christ to steer us in the direction of Himself!

We will always find ourselves in need of God. His everlasting goodness, compared to the conditional state of our lives, reveals Him as the only anchor for our wondering souls. Though our heart and strength my fail us, His love is all we need. So we must lean on God's word and adhere to the wisdom of those He has placed over our lives. We must exercise our faith in God's goodness, even in the midst of our fears. The frailty of our existence requires that we place our hope, our faith and our trust in Him alone, because anything else will eventually dissatisfy and leave us defenseless in the face of fear.

Drawing Near

I didn't receive my driver's license until I was nineteen years old. (Don't laugh!) I held off taking the permit class until the fall of my senior year of high school, and then I prolonged taking the actual driver's course with great avoidance. My parents kept urging me to take the test, but I was in no hurry to do so. It was two months after I graduated before I even dared to make an appointment at the DMV.

The experience was terrifying and I failed the road test *three* times. I could hear the commands from the driving instructor, but I couldn't seem to follow them. I ran a red light and a few stop signs. I couldn't seem to stay in my lane. Tractor trucks intimidated me, and once, I think I even closed my eyes in overwhelming anxiety! Oh, gosh! I'm embarrassed to even admit this! I felt so defeated that I almost didn't bother to make the fourth attempt.

Fear was behind all the delays and hindrances to getting my license. During my sophomore year of high school, we lost four students in a car crash. They were all driving home together, and unfortunately, none survived the impact. It was devastating. Our school sank into a somber mood for weeks following. One of the girls who died had sat right in front of me in biology class. Her empty seat was never filled and I was left with great apprehension over getting behind the wheel of a car by myself. What if I got into a wreck? What if I got hurt in a car crash?

Too often, we become so paranoid over the "what-ifs" in life that we become immobile. The Lord seeks to take us places, and faith is necessary to maneuver with Him on the journey. Our fears definitely will hinder our progress and prolong our arrival into the mission and destinies He's crafting for us to accomplish. We can't go anywhere or move anything without faith.

In Matthew 17:20, Jesus' disciples were confused because they were unable to drive out an evil spirit. They said to Jesus, "We tried to remove it, but it wouldn't go. Why couldn't we drive it out?" Jesus said back, *"Because you have so little faith. Truly I tell you, if you have faith as small as a mustard seed, you can say to this mountain, 'Move from here to there,' and it will move. Nothing will be impossible for you"* (NIV).

The idea of being anywhere near a demon is some pretty scary stuff! Thank goodness most of us aren't called to perform exorcisms, but we know that the power of darkness is at work all around us, and this darkness can be the cause of fears that we sometimes face. According to The New Unger's Bible Dictionary, demons are unclean spirits.* By their nature, they aggravate and instigate fear in our lives and in our hearts. Fear itself is a spirit. And spirits of fear work in ways completely contrary to God's Word. But Scripture tells us that, *"God has not given us the spirit of fear, but of power, love and a sound mind"* (2 Timothy 1:7 NKJV). God desires to destroy the fear that enables us to move. We come across the phrase "fear not" 365 times throughout the Bible. That's one reminder for every day of the year!

---

* Merrill F. Unger, *The New Unger's Bible Dictionary*, (Chicago, IL: Moody Bible Institute, 1988), 298.

Faith in faith alone has no power over fear. Since fear is spiritual, our faith must derive from God's Spirit. Christ made it clear to the disciples in Mark 9:23, and He insists the same is true for you: *"All things are possible for one who believes"* (ESV). It takes only a little faith to do big things! Our failure to surrender our fears to God is actually an admission of distrust. We clench for control, yet Christ calls us to believe He is who He says He is—in His word and in our lives. Hebrews 10:22 says, *"Let us draw near to God with a sincere heart and with the full assurance that faith brings"* (NIV).

Assurance is produced by faith because it draws us closer to Christ. What do we have to fear if we are in Him? As we seek Him, through the reading of His word and through prayer, He shows us that He is love and in His love we have confidence in all that we face. We don't need to cower in fear because He is with us. Don't believe the lies of fear! *"We are more than conquerors through Him who loved us,"* (Romans 8:37 NIV)! His love makes us brave! Know that as we place our trust in Him our faith will increase as we experience His presence through faith and prayer.

In my Bible I have a quote from one of my dad's old sermons. He said, *"Prayer is not a tool to change God's mind; it is God's gift to change our hearts in His holy presence."* Through prayer, we access God's presence. And who should we fear if He is near? If we aren't on our knees lifting things to God, we likely have positioned ourselves to lift up our circumstances, our concerns, and our worries above Him. Putting focus on what causes us to worry, inevitably invites fear, because if we're honest, we aren't in control of anything. We never have been and we never will be. Christ holds it all in His hands. If we are not consistently exercising our faith by drawing near to Him, then fear will eventually consume us and alter us unrecognizable. Fear holds us captive and prevents us from going forth and doing what God has called us to do. It paralyzes us and prevents us from moving forward.

In contrast, our faith, when placed not in ourselves but in the Lord, ignites us to take action and sustains us throughout the difficulties of this life. If we expect to see God's goodness in our lives, we must keep the doors of communication open through faith and prayer. This is not accomplished with radical displays or emotional experiences. We simply need to hand all of our fears to the only One who can handle them. *"Draw near to God and He will draw near to you,"* James 4:8 says. Our confidence fades in the shadow of fear, but our courage increases when we are close to God and draw near to Him by living in obedience and agreement with His word.

True faith obeys God even when we aren't quite sure that we believe. Just as God commanded Joshua, He also says to you, *"Be strong and very courageous... Do not be afraid or discouraged. For the Lord your God is with you wherever you go"* (Joshua 1:7-9 NLT).

In my life, I have come across families whose lives have changed completely simply because they had faith. In church, I've heard stories about healings and restoration, which came not as a result of monumental feats but from quiet prayers and silent tears. In my own life, I am learning that fear can seem so big, but our seemingly small faith becomes giants in the hands of our powerful God! In our prayers, our faith is strengthened and strong faith eliminates weakness from fear. Prayer invites God's presence into every situation and circumstance, and His presence drives out all fear.

Quiet in the Storm

I attended a small Lutheran school for my elementary and middle school education and one of our assignments was to look up the meaning of our names. My name means "purity." And I love this meaning so much. There was no way my mother could have known how seriously I would take the meaning of my name. Even before I knew what my name meant, I had committed myself to sexual purity at age twelve. Living in purity through abstinence until marriage or celibacy in singlehood is a powerful state in which to live. It makes a loud statement. It shocks people. It gives you a platform to share Jesus. I've always loved my name, and my love for it grew more after I found out its meaning.

My family calls me "Trina," but as I grew older, I felt so poised and grown up when I heard "Katrina." So, you can imagine why I was completely devastated when they decided to give the New Orleans hurricane, this name. This hurricane was one of the most economically draining natural disasters the United States has ever endured. The storm has been ranked as the third most intense United States tropical cyclone ever to make landfall, and ranked behind only the 1935 Labor Day hurricane and Hurricane Camille of 1969.*

Today, many people still deal with devastation as a result of Hurricane Katrina. It tore portions of our country apart, but it also brought thousands of people together. My friend Kourtney selflessly chose to volunteer during her spring break for a mission trip to help with the cleanup. She was truly humbled by the experience and has shared many stories with me about the communities she served there. Hurricane Katrina was truly cataclysmic; it shattered a number of lives and communities. Storms have a way of doing that. It's their unpredictability that makes them so devastating.

In a parallel, we each face our share of spiritual storms as well.

---

* Charles River Editors, *Hurricane Katrina: the Story of the Most Destructive Hurricane in American History* (North Charleston: CreateSpace, 2014), 5.

Storms can be humbling agents. We all go through them from time to time. The catastrophe can be life altering, but every storm serves the purpose of deepening our dependence and relationship with the Lord. In a storm, people prepare, people pray, and people are afraid. Sometimes storms make us evacuate our houses to prevent possible fatalities. One and a half million people had to evacuate New Orleans.* They left their lives and homes behind without knowing how the storm would affect all that they'd held dear. Though perhaps ignited by fear, it was an act of faith for those families to drop everything and go. Sometimes Christ asks us to do the same in our lives: drop everything and go. In our spiritual storms, we have to let faith compel us to leave behind our pride, doubts, excuses, and all sin that weighs us down. Evacuation requires abandonment. Certain things we can't take with us.

Hurricane Karina took place in 2005. Twelve years later, I am still reminded of that storm every now and then, simply at the mention of my name. Once, at the bank, as I was handing over my card, the clerk said he felt sorry for me and asked me if I still liked my name. I was quite annoyed. I've had people ask me if I'd consider a name change and I've been the brunt of many hurricane jokes. On a recent interview, the supervisor asked me if I had a temper like the hurricane. Not funny. People have asked me, "How does it feel to be named after a storm?" I'm always shocked at this question because I am clearly older than twelve years old. But people tend to identify you with reflections from the past. Sometimes, the memory of storms can linger.

Jesus, too, found Himself in a storm. In Mark chapter 4, we read about a storm which led the disciples into a panic. They were frantic

---

* Gary Rivlin, *Katrina: After the Flood* (New York: Simon & Schuster Paperbacks, 2016), 6.

with fear and ready to drop their plans, evacuate, and head back home. The Bible says that the high and ferocious waves were filling the boat with water. Drowning is a great fear, and scripture makes it obvious that the disciples were reacting to this fear with anxiety and irrational responses. I suspect they were probably yelling and blaming each other over the waves. And since Peter was on the boat, there were probably plenty of swear words thrown around, as well! So, where was Jesus in all of this commotion? Well, of course, you know... He was sleeping through it all!

> *"Jesus was in the stern, sleeping on a cushion. The disciples woke him and said to him, 'Teacher, don't you care if we drown?' He got up, rebuked the wind and said to the waves, 'Quiet! Be still!' Then the wind died down, and it was completely calm. He said to his disciples, 'Why are you so afraid? Do you still have no faith?' They were terrified and asked each other, 'Who is this? Even the wind and the waves obey him'"* (Mark 4:38-41 NIV).

This story was my morning reading today. As I read this scripture, the Lord brought to my heart that maybe He was speaking to both the disciples and the waves at the same time when He said, "Quiet!" At this moment in my life, I'm dealing with a storm of my own. Maybe you are, too. Storms can be scary when faced alone, and I am an easily excitable person! In my storm, I feel overwhelmed, but I know I'm not alone. Even though I feel as if the seas of fear could drown me, in my heart, I know Christ is my rescuer! I'm learning to keep my eyes on Him and not the waves.

My husband told me that when he was small, his grandma would make him be quiet during a storm. They'd turn out all of the lights and sit still. No one would talk or move until the storm was over or until they went to sleep. We dealt with storms a bit differently in my house. My brother and I would jump into each other's beds or jump into bed with my parents. If the thunder was loud, I would scream! I would pull the covers over my head and sing loud songs to combat the noise outside and my fears within. My mom would tickle us and we'd have yelling matches to drown out the noises that surrounded us. Inside our house, we were just as loud as the calamity going on outside!

When we find ourselves in storms, we can react in one of two ways: we can let fear lead us and let our attitudes and actions reflect the chaos of the storm we're facing, or we can exercise our faith by trusting God through those waves while He quiets them down for us. When we are operating in fear, we cannot hear from the Lord. Our fear resounds too loudly for our hearts to discern God's instructions and leading. But we can heed Psalm 46:10, *"Be still and know that I am God"(*ESV*).* This doesn't mean that we'll never face things that are scary; it just means we can develop faith in Christ and prevent our fears from overtaking us.

Hurricane Katrina was a natural and national disaster. Dozens of families are still in the process of recovery. They desperately need our prayers, encouragement, and support. They need to know that they've not been forgotten. But, in spite of the horrific aftermath, many positive outcomes followed the storm. According to Slate Magazine, *"This gave New Orleans an unprecedented opportunity to remake a city that wasn't working."* Entrepreneurship increased, neighborhoods got cleaned up, race relations improved and crime rates decreased. A 2010 Pew poll reflected that residents became more optimistic concerning New Orleans' progress in rebuilding a stronger and more inclusive community with offices and malls as well as in people's lives and futures.* This type of reconstruction went far beyond better levees and floodwalls.

I remember watching Jack Van Impe with my parents as he and his wife were discussing their take on the storm. He said there was a reason why God impressed it on people's hearts to name the storm, "Katrina", because purity comes from washing away interferences. Out of the chaos, so much healing and restoration came about. I so want that for myself: God washing away any interference in my life that might keep me from Him! Christ uses the disarray from tragedies to show us what needs to be cleaned up in our hearts. Every storm serves a purpose.

I continually pray for the people of New Orleans, and I celebrate the beauty that is being restored to their community. During a storm, things get destroyed, but out of the destruction, new opportunities arise! Restoration only occurs through brokenness, so God is continually rebuilding His beauty within us, through the washing of His love and His word. Sometimes it takes a storm to accomplish restoration. Our souls can find rest in our storms when we trust Jesus. We don't have to be afraid. Storms are unpredictable and loud and messy. But in the wind and the waves, we don't have to fear because Jesus is in our boat. And He has the power to soothe our souls by telling the storms, and our hearts, to "Be quiet."

---

* Juan Williams, "Even Katrina Has a Silver Lining," *Fox News Opinion,* August 27, 2010, Accessed March 1, 2015, http://www.foxnews.com/opinion/2010/08/27/juan-williams-katrina-brookings-new-orleans-gulf-coast-black-poverty-pew-poll.html.

Laying it Down

I was recently asked, "If you had all the resources needed to be successful in your dreams, what would you be doing right now?" My first thought was, "I'd be making plans to publish the book I'm writing." What might your dreams be?

I believe God has placed dreams within each of us to inspire us. Our dreams reflect God's creativity. They keep us praying and meditating upon His promises. They fill us with a purpose in the present and hope for the future. We are all "dreamers," and we are each filled with aspirations for our dreams to come true. Dreams come to us in moments of joy and produce anticipation, determination, and concentration in our lives. They can truly be a Godsend! But the fulfillment of our dreams isn't intended to satisfy us. We are blessed to be a blessing, and the fruit of our accomplishments should sow seeds in the lives of others. If you are the only person who benefits from your desires, then beware of the spirit of selfishness. If your goals and aspirations are set in motion for your benefit only, then I challenge you to check the motivations and intentions of your heart. Consider the prayers you are praying. Is there anyone else who might benefit should God answer them?

In our culture, self-fulfillment can appear glorious, but so often it ends in self-deprivation. We can miss out on what God truly has for us when we focus inwardly. This tendency is why scripture tells us to seek God's pleasure and His kingdom first (Matthew 6:33). This seeking is the blueprint for true success and the motive to awaken dreams that leave legacies! If we aren't positioning ourselves to serve God with our dreams, then we are only investing in temporal things instead of what's eternal. We must be careful that our dreams do not become our gods.

I think one of the most beautiful and controversial stories in the Bible is the one about Isaac. His birth was a promise to Abraham. Although his father made some tragic mistakes which still affect the world today, God honored Abraham's faithful heart by keeping His Word. He blessed Abraham with a son.

> *"Now the Lord was gracious to Sarah as he had said, and the Lord did for Sarah what he had promised. Sarah became pregnant and bore a son to Abraham in his old age, at the very time God had promised him. Abraham gave the name Isaac to the son Sarah bore him. When his son Isaac was eight days old, Abraham circumcised him, as God commanded him. Abraham was a hundred years old when his son Isaac was born to him"* (Genesis 21:1-5 NIV).

I think it's safe to say that, at around the age of ninety-nine years old, Abraham might have had some fears that his dreams would never come to fruition. This fear is probably why he and his wife, Sarah, tried to take their dreams into their own hands by producing Ishmael (see Genesis 16:1-4). Ishmael, although blessed by God to be a prince, was a threat to the promise of Isaac that God had made to Sarah and Abraham. Ishmael's creation came out of unbelief. Though Abraham and Sarah were successful in their plans to birth him, his existence produced a lack of peace which eventually gave way to fear. If we are honest, many of us can attest that sometimes our dreams perpetuate our fears.

Each of our lives have mission. We must use the light of scripture to view our desires in order to keep our motives in line with each unique assignment God has placed over us. If a desire lines up with scripture, we can walk in confidence in pursuit of it. But fear displays itself when we reach to control our dreams, hopes, and aspirations instead of entrusting the outcomes to God. Selfish ambition does not produce faithfulness to Christ's will or good spiritual fruit. I have come across many young women who have dreams of this or that and fall prey to being led astray simply because they were unable or unwilling to consult God concerning their vision. Just because you have a desire doesn't mean God will fulfill it in your way or your timing. If He isn't the one leading your course as you pursue your dreams, those aspirations could become a distraction to the very course that God has designed for you.

The best way to gauge this is to consider what your response would be if the Lord asked you to lay something down. Would you be willing to call it quits if the Lord asked it of you? Would you be willing to accept a "no" to having children or receiving a raise? Would you be willing to stay single for the rest of your life? Would you have peace if God said, "no" to your prayers for physical healing? Our reaction to God's "no" is always a reflection of our faith.

Dreams help us keep hoping, but we cannot make the mistake of placing our hope in our dreams. These aren't what sustain us—only God can do that. My dream to write a book first came to my heart almost five years ago. Abraham waited one hundred years for Isaac. You are waiting, too, but in your waiting are you finding faith or entertaining fear?

Abraham was afraid of not having the miracle son God had promised, so out of control and self-effort, he made Ishmael. Ishmael later became a source of fear for both Abraham and Sarah. He threatened the dream that God eventually brought forth. Isaac was a blessing, but God still required Abraham to choose between his dream or his God.

> *"After these things God tested Abraham and said to him, 'Abraham!' And he said, 'Here I am.' He said, 'Take your son, your only son Isaac, whom you love, and go to the land of Moriah, and offer him there as a burnt offering on one of the mountains of which I shall tell you.' So Abraham rose early in the morning, saddled his donkey, and took two of his young men with him, and his son Isaac"* (Genesis 22: 1-3 ESV).

Again, our dreams are not meant to sustain us. They are meant to bear witness to the goodness and glory of God. If we are too focused on our dreams, we'll find ourselves in great fear when God asks us to hand them over to Him. Our dreams are special, but they are not sacred. We have to be sure that our faith is in God because one day, He will require us to lay down anything that we have placed above Him.

When that moment comes, and it will come, will we be women who operate in faith or fear? Fear says, "Lord, make a way because my dreams are what I trust." Faith says, "Lord, I trust you with my dreams, so I know you will make a way."

Nothing that God has promised can be undone. The purpose of your dream is to cultivate your growth and faith in Him as the One who'll bring those dreams into reality. We have no guarantee of the outcome, but we are guaranteed that God has only good things in store for those who love Him. As Romans 8:28 states, *"And we know that God causes all things to work together for good to those who love God, to those who are called according to His purpose"* (NASB). He is faithful and can be trusted with the intimate desires of our hearts! Those dreams you pray over just might be His vision for your calling. Those desires you meditate on might reflect exactly who God wants you to become; maybe so... maybe not. Only He knows. But I promise, as we seek Him, pursue Him, desire more of Him, and spend more of ourselves on Him, His vision for each of us will become clearer and clearer. Our hearts will start to align with His! This union of heart and mind is my prayer for you. This union is also my prayer for myself and for every woman that comes after us. May we be women of faith who trust God with our dreams.

Learning to "let go and let God" takes a lifetime of practice. Each season of experience comes with its own dreams, desires, struggles, and fears, which are essential in developing our faith in God and His mission over us. Laying down our dreams requires real faith. Doing so frees us from our own control and our own sense of what is perfect. We will never be in the position of producing perfection, as we'd only create a platform of self-righteousness. Our position must always be submission to God's love and His goodness. He is the accomplisher! Not you, and not me. We can't do anything in ourselves but assume things, worry, and complain. This is not freedom and this mindset is not our calling. Nothing is accidental. God has placed hopes and desires within us on purpose, but they haven't been placed in our lives for us to take control. They require our faith. Psalm 20:4 is true: *"May he give you the desire of your heart and make all your plans succeed"* (NIV).

Never stop dreaming! Never be ashamed of the desires that you long for or the secret prayers you pray over your future and your destiny! Our dreams stem from God's purposes for us. Just as God produced a dream within Abraham, He has things to call forth within you, as well. As you pursue your goals, seek God first and the accomplishment of His work in you! Trust Him, and have no fear. Honor Him, and you will be blessed. Seek Him, and doors will open! God's questions to you are the same as His questions were to Abraham: "*Will you offer it up to Me? Will you believe Me with your whole heart? Do you believe that My freedom is greater than your fears? Do you choose Me over your dreams?"*

Doubting our Doubts

There's a blog I enjoy following that has frequent advertisements for personality quizzes. I've taken them once or twice, as humor really, and each time, I've ended up with different results. I guess it just depends on the day. I'm a very outgoing person when I'm comfortable. When I'm with my family and close friends, I am jovial and hilarious! I'm quite enthusiastic and wild in my disposition and I enjoy making a scene! But, when I find myself around unfamiliar territory or intimidating environments, I become introverted and hesitant— afraid to be myself simply out of uncertainty for how I will be accepted or perceived. It's like my worries hold my personality hostage, and I'm left feeling awkward and dumb.

Many of us are so confident on the outside but extremely fragile on the inside. We question our abilities, and ourselves and if we are honest, we latch on to the first thing that makes us feel good because, well,...it feels good! We don't always step up to our challenges. Our safety nets hinder us and hold us back. Confidence in ourselves is circumstantial and can be easily manipulated by external doubts and fears. In our comfort zones, we are undefeatable, but in our areas of challenge, we tend to cave into solitudes of uncertainty. Doubt finds a way to adorn us like tacky jewelry, so we try to tuck it out of sight in hopes no one notices. The enemy of our soul loves sowing seeds of doubt. Because we have the victory in Christ, he cannot take anything from us. His greatest weapon is through deception, causing us to shake on our stance in faith. Though he is successful at times, we can overcome in victory by aligning our thoughts and actions with the Word of God. My brother Ben has said many times, "We must believe our beliefs and doubt our doubts."

Doubt is an open invitation to lies. It is a sure fire way to get us off course. Scripture tells us that the enemy comes to *"steal, kill and destroy"* all the hopes, dreams, freedom, and victory that are ours in Christ (John 10:10 NIV). Even our very lives are targeted for destruction by the evil one. But he is a defeated foe (Luke 10:19). He's only successful when we ponder his lies instead of God's promises. That's really all that doubt is: it is the confusion that surfaces when we temporarily believe an untruth over what is consistently true. We each have to learn how to cast our adversary down!

Belief is a blessed gift. It's the spiritual confidence that powerfully declares that our God is true, trustworthy, and good! I love what Luke 1:45 says about Mary, the mother of Jesus: *"Blessed is she who has believed that the Lord would fulfill his promises to her!"* (NIV). Her belief gave her confidence. And confidence helps remove any room for doubt. Without confidence, fear settles in our hearts. We are afraid of what we don't understand, what we can't control, and what we don't feel comfortable with. But Christ is seeking to develop our faith in the midst of our fears. He is inviting us to trust Him and come closer to Him with everything we hold.

Our unbelief, even in the smallest of areas, causes us to question God. It put us in the same predicament Eve faced in the garden in Genesis 3:1-7. She knew what God had said. She was aware of the risks of disobedience, but instead of casting down the deceiver, she engaged in conversation with the master of lies. She invited doubt into her mind, and as a result, the enemy poisoned her thoughts toward God and His promises over her. She trusted an unfamiliar spirit over the

God she knew and her temporary doubts soon turned into permanent fears. Consequently, Adam and Eve hid from God's presence, due to doubt and fear, and admitted that they felt frightened of the Lord (Genesis 3:10). Their doubts deprived them of their capacity for faith.

But unlike the first man and woman, we have Christ indwelling us. We have the presence of the Lord within us in every circumstance and we've witnessed His goodness firsthand! Our faith is strengthened by our experiences in Christ and the personal testimonies of others about God's love and faithfulness. Nothing He gives us is circumstantial or temporary. We can choose not to doubt, because He is ever consistent with who He says He is and who He says we are before Him. God asks us to have faith in His faithfulness. He increases our faith as we choose to believe Him!

Remember, we are each purposed to be impactful! To be family changers, community changers, and world changers requires a measure of faith enough to eliminate our fears. Will we be uncertain at times? Of course! Will we be timid and shy and sometimes scared? Yes, we will. But as we believe God and focus on His leading, we combat fear every step of the way. Fear binds us; faith releases us. Our faith comes through believing the truth of God. And the truth shall set us free! It's our desire to become women of faith and of courage. Just like Mary, we must learn to position our hearts to believe what God is saying. Our responses will reflect our relationship of trust in Him. We can choose to believe and be blessed because we know God's promises are true and each one is for our soul's good. Nothing He has in store is evil (Hebrews 10:20-21), so each and every promise of God should be worn like tattoos on our hearts—as permanent reminders of His goodness and His unconditional love for us. 1 John 4:18 declares, *"There is no fear in love. But perfect love drives out fear"* (NIV).

Listen ladies, if our hearts are aligned with Christ, blessings will come as a result of our belief. Fear and doubt have no place, so we must bind these up in Jesus' name! We are called by our all-powerful and eternal God to walk in continual confidence and have no fear, because the glory of His presence surrounds us daily. We don't need to distress! We are equipped for any battle, challenge, and storm because He has branded us with His very own identity of love (1 John 4:8). Do we believe that? We must, or otherwise our doubts will consume us.

Yes and No

God's goodness and not our own, is the basis for the production of faith required to combat our fears. We trust God because He is good! For our faith to produce fruit, we must deal honestly with ourselves so that we properly perceive God's goodness and love for us. Do we know that we are loved even when things don't turn out our way? Do we trust God when our prayers don't result in the specific answers we've asked for? These are important questions to ponder, because so many times, our faith dissipates when we don't get our way. Yet, we are still loved and God is still good! Our acceptance of this is the first step of faith.

The Lord desires to perfect His goodness and His love in us for His glory with all that He has declared over our hearts. He has proven Himself over and over again in His word and in the confirmation of examples that we've witnessed in the lives of others. It's easy to misunderstand what faith in Christ really means. This spiritual method is not something we use to manipulate God to do what we want Him to do, in the way we want Him to do it; rather it is a gift that He produces in us to strengthen our hearts during every result He cultivates in our lives. Let's get real: not every prayer we pray will result in the outcome we desire. Even with all the faith in the universe, there will be some answers we receive from the Lord that won't align with what we ask for. Yes, our God is able and our God can do anything! There is nothing too difficult or beyond His ability. But just because He *can* doesn't always mean that He will. So our faith is not based on God appeasing us in all that we request. Our faith is truly shown in our willingness to trust Him no matter the outcome of His will.

When my husband and I found out we were pregnant, a very gracious decision was made to allow me to stay home with our newborn daughter for her first year; it was one of the most precious moments of my life! During this time, I completed my Master's program, online, and began writing this book. After almost eighteen comfortable months at home, it was time to go back to work, so I accepted a part time teaching position at one of the community colleges in our area. The position called for an instructor of English for international students. How exciting, right? But, my first day on the job was horrific! The pampering by makeup artists and wardrobe stylists were far away, and I questioned whether I could even make it through my first day as the ESL instructor for the Aston Woods Refugee community.

On paper, the position seemed like a dream! I was so excited to get started—it seemed so exotic and eclectic! I imagined myself changing the world and inspiring foreigners with the American dream by providing them with the richness of a free education. But, I soon discovered that the environment I had imagined was far from inspirational. Not only was my classroom off campus, the department decided not to provide me with a translator or even books, due to budget shortages. A little apartment, in the refugee community, had been transformed into a makeshift classroom and shared a property with the neighborhood trash dump. The whiff of urine from a broken toilet saturated the air inside, and I remember coughing upon entering the room. I hadn't had the opportunity to visit the site beforehand, but I had purchased some plug-in air fresheners from Bath and Body Works to give the room a sweet aroma for my new students. You all probably know what happens when you try to combine sweet smells with ghastly ones…well, now I know, too! The funk was funky!

Hot tears swelled in my eyes and anxiety overcame me. I was surrounded by discomfort and, to my dismay, the urine wasn't the only problem I faced that first morning. Dozens… and I mean dozens of roaches greeted me from every corner! It was the middle of August and there was no air conditioning, either. Did I mention there were roaches? Lots of roaches— *everywhere*! They were the big flying kind that refuse to die. They would fall from the ceiling and scatter as they hit the floor. One fell on my sandal! They would crawl over to the white board as I attempted to write a "good morning" message for my students. I about lost my whole entire life! I cringe just thinking about it! In addition, I was also deeply disappointed because I had planned to play instrumental music to set a welcoming ambiance for my students, but there was no internet available. I should have stopped for coffee! #longday!

One by one, adult students from parts of the world I had never heard of, walked into the little classroom. There was a great divide between the scholastic abilities of each individual, so lesson differentiation was an obvious challenge for me. On that first day, most of the students had no shoes on, and hygiene presented an immediate concern. No one spoke English, and I didn't speak Swahili or Arabic. Who would have known a community like this even existed in North Carolina? I was completely out of my comfort zone and was definitely a long, long way from the glamor of modeling studios! I tried to great each person with smiles, but no one smiled back because no one knew what I was saying. Intimidation filled my heart profusely, and my head spun round as anxiety rose within me. I had no colleagues to consult, no teacher's assistant, no supply of paper, and no books. I was alone and unprepared. "Hmm", I thought, "let's begin with the alphabet...Jesus, help me!"

Fear is real. It intimidates and unnerves us, but our faith can bring us through victoriously. Faith in Jesus will cause us to shine brightly like the morning! No matter what we face or where we might find ourselves, we have the confidence and courage necessary to face any fear because God is within us! He doesn't just limit Himself to walk with us side by side, He *resides* inside of us and fills us with the necessary strength required for the tasks He entrusts us with. *"God is within her, she will not fail; God will help her at break of day."* (Psalm 46:5 NIV)

On my first day on this particular job, I knew I needed some serious courage. On my own and in my own strength, I didn't have what it took to be successful, so I depended greatly on The Lord. To be honest, the job I truly wanted was much more glamorous and desirable than the one I accepted. I had signed a contract with a small agency six months before I had accepted the ESL position. I'd prayed that God would open up doors for me to do some catalog modeling and I truly believed that He would. Why not? He'd given me success before and I was a very talented model. It only made sense that this request would be answered in my favor. C'mon, it wasn't even serious modeling. Yet, every time my agent would send me to an audition, high hopes were met with disappointment. For the entire six months, I failed to book any jobs—not even one! It was difficult accepting the reality of no modeling work, as prior to marriage, I'd seen a very thriving career. I'd traveled to some of the biggest cities and walked for some well-established designers. Why wasn't I doing so well with this local contract? I was discouraged, so I began to look for more practical job opportunities where I could utilize my degree. This search led me to the ESL position and although it wasn't what I expected, in any way, shape or form, the experience was all part of God's plan in building me and my dependence on Him.

As I look back, I realize that the Lord's "no" to local modeling was necessary for His "yes" toward my new career, teaching refugees and growing confidence in public speaking. Had I cowered and stopped after my first day with the creepy-crawlies, I would have missed the joy I found from teaching my sweet students. I would have missed the enthusiasm and creativity that developed within me as I worked to help downcast people come into greatness. As a result of this experience, I've seen some of my students move out of the program and onto a college campus. I've seen the shy and intimidated ones stand up in front of everyone and read out loud with pride and confidence! My class has grown in numbers and I've found more fulfillments in that tiny apartment teaching foreigners and strangers than I've ever had in any other job. And I praise God that the exterminator now visits us twice a month! Bye-bye bugs!

Life brings about some scary stuff and sometimes things don't work out according to the way we pray. We aren't promised a life with out problems, but we are promised a God who loves us and will never leave us (Matthew 28:20). So we must keep the faith! Whether we are experiencing seasons of prosperity and positive outcomes or we feel as if we are going through hell, God is there. He desires that we trust Him because He knows what He is doing and where He is taking us.

He will not let us fail. His dealings are only for our best, so in the "yes's" and in the "no's" we get in life, we can know we are dearly loved and that God's responses to our every desire and need are better than what we could have ever imagined (Ephesians 3:20).

Having faith isn't about finagling God to give us our way; it's about trusting Him and celebrating the fact that He will have His way in each of us in His timing and for His purposes, which are ultimately for our good. Whether we're in the valley or on the mountaintop, Christ desires to perfect our faith in Him. Fear hinders us. Faith frees us. Fear is conditional. Faith defies outward conditions. Nothing we go through is accidental, so we can move forward with the confidence of Christ, knowing that we will succeed in Him! His ways are always better and His plans are far more illustrious than ours will ever be. Remember, God won't put you in places you won't ultimately overcome. *"We are more than conquerors through Him who loved us,"* Romans 8:37 states (ESV). It's by our faith in God's promises and in His word that we overcome feelings of fear! We have no guarantees in this life, but we know that *"Christ will never leave us nor forsake us,"* (Hebrews 13:5 ESV).

My prayer for us all is that we will always be women who embrace the heights of Christ's love for us. May we begin to believe with our hearts and not just our heads. We will definitely mess up and fear will sometimes get in our way. There will always be gossip to avoid, cuss words to apologize for, temptations of every kind to tackle and forgiveness to be granted and received. Never apologize for your humanity. We serve a Savior who is accustomed and who understands our weaknesses and struggles (Hebrews 4:15). And though we sometimes feel intimidated in our own strength, Christ has equipped us to victory, with a mission of His love. These things propel us onward in the faith and enable us to cast down our fears. The greater our faith, through our continued experience in God's love, the more we move in victory over doubt and fear!

I honestly hope I am blessing someone with these truths. I'm blessing myself as I write because, to be honest, I have been walking in moments of fear for the past few months. At times, it seems these fears might overcome me, but they won't. They simply can't because of Romans 8:31. It states, *"If God is on our side, who can ever be against us?"* (TLB). We don't have to set the table for fear because it's an unwelcome guest. We have the power and authority to insist that it leave by inviting God's presence in stead. He longs to be near to us, in every thing we face. He won't desert us in a valley of fear. Though, sometimes, things don't work out according to the way we pray, that's ok, because God's plans are perfect. We can't always determine the outcome of God's will, but we do know that He will lead us safely and successfully into our destiny. His answer won't always be "yes," but His process will continuously develop us into our greatness for His glory! Even His "no's" are for our good. So, we don't have to be afraid.

Questions for Discussion

1. Reflect on a time in your life when you were afraid. Was it in a family crisis or when you faced personal intimidation? How were you able to experience God's love in that "storm?"

2. Record Matthew 28:20 Below.

   How can this verse give you hope and faith in spite of your fears?

3. Have you ever experienced a disappointment by a "no" response to a prayer, only to be thankful for the results? How did this experience growth your faith?

CHAPTER 8

The Beauty of Rejection

One night, while tossing in bed, I kept having dreadful thoughts, which turned into frustrations, which turned into a heartfelt prayer to God.

"Lord, you know I keep trying to love, but I'm tired of reaching out to her. Nothing seems to be getting better. I don't want to do it anymore. I'm done! Amen".

We all have a deep desire for relationships in our lives. We want meaningful connections, and we want to feel appreciated. It's human to have this heart's desire because God, who is spirit, created our spirits to be like His. He is a relational God, so it only makes sense that He'd give us this longing for relationship, as well. So, with sincere hearts, we offer our friendship and give of our time. We extend ourselves with good intentions, and, out of naïve assumptions, we expect the same in return. But the truth is, acceptance is never guaranteed, even if your motives are pure.

Each of us have experienced some form of rejection in our lives. It can be disheartening, as we're never prepared for a negative response to our genuine kindness. Rejections are a part of life, but no one ever sees them coming. We're not given an allotment of time to plan for disappointment or heartbreak. We're never prepared for unkindness or disrespect, yet Christ warns us to expect such treatment from others. Know that there is a blessing for you because of it (Matthew 5:11). It's so hard to accept though, isn't it? The impacts of such negative experiences can be quite devastating; producing a spiritual war within us: do we keep on loving, or do we reject those who have rejected us?

Love is the Mission

Keep in mind that every encounter with someone is our opportunity to share Jesus, but not every person will come to salvation as a result of what we share. Our message won't always be welcomed with open arms. I think, sometimes, people mistake God's perfect love flowing through us to be personal perfection within us. This can make them angry, because they don't understand. It is our mission to share God's love, but it won't always be returned with smiles and gratitude, especially from those who do not desire a relationship with Christ. It can be disheartening and tiresome, and that's ok, because giving love is never about us; it's about serving Jesus. We were never promised a life free from hurts or rejections. We already know that trouble and problems come automatically in this world and even more so to those committed to following Christ (John 16:33). But, if we reject those who've hurt us or avoid the discomfort of loving unkind people, then we miss the crux of the matter. Our lives are not our own; we are to live them as displays in the physical of what God has done for us in the spiritual.

Loving others can be a challenge, especially when we face seemingly dead situations. Our initial choice might be to give up, but Jesus is Lord even over the dead! In the book of John Chapter 11, Jesus resurrected Lazarus back to life. He called him back from the grave after four days.

Several people witnessed this miracle and then ate dinner with Lazarus afterward! But you know what? One day, Lazarus died again. Our flesh is corruptible; it's not meant to last forever in this fallen world. Sometimes, it's easier to view situations from a carnal perspective instead of a spiritual one. But when we've been hurt, and kindness seems difficult, Jesus can resurrect our capacity to love and restore life to our wounded hearts. Medical doctors can revitalize a physical heart to beat again. This is science. But the resurrection of a dead soul...wow! Only Jesus Christ can do that! He can grace us to show the world what the mission of love truly looks like, even in the impossible.

Remember, there is no blessing in fighting fire with fire or returning unkindness with unkindness. Shade for shade is ineffective. This is the way the enemy operates, and in the long run, it's self-devouring and unproductive for Kingdom work.

> "*If you love those who love you, what credit is that to you? Even sinners love those who love them. And if you do good to those who are good to you, what credit is that to you? Even sinners do that. And if you lend to those from whom you expect repayment, what credit is that to you? Even sinners lend to sinners, expecting to be repaid in full. But love your enemies, do good to them, and lend to them without expecting to get anything back. Then your reward will be great, and you will be children of the Most High, because He is kind to the ungrateful and wicked. Be merciful, just as your Father is merciful*" (Luke 6:33 NIV).

We forgive our transgressors because holding onto resentment won't produce the goodness of God within us. The enemy wants us to operate in sin against God; he wants to spoil the integrity of our hearts and distract us with unkindness. But God constantly forgives us over and over again, so we must do the same for others. This can be so difficult—I know! It can feel so disheartening, so belittling and very unfair. But in God's Word, we are told that, *"The Lord is close to the brokenhearted and saves those who are crushed in spirit"* (Psalm 34:18 NIV). He is always with us, even when we find it difficult to be like Him.

No matter what we face, we must remember that this life in Christ is not based on our abilities. We can't rely on our flesh to show Jesus. Our feelings are irrelevant if they conflict with what scripture tells us. In John 14:15, Jesus said, *"If you love me, show it by doing what I've told you"* (MSG). He did not say, "If you love me, you can do what I've told you when you feel comfortable." If we love Him, then we obey. Period. We love those who hurt us simply because Christ has asked us to. He desires to show them a love that they can't explain, just as He's shown us a love that we will never comprehend. When we love like Christ, we become free like Christ. As we forgive, God fashions the beauty of His love within us and His love is strong enough to cover *"a broken and contrite heart"* (Psalm 51:17 ESV).

Rejection is shattering, but God can produce beauty within us as we turn our devastation over to Him and allow His love to heal us and flow through us. His love is a powerful tool! It's not chocolate and roses and butterfly kisses —it's a spiritual weapon that breaks down walls and frees our souls. There is a beauty in rejection, only when we focus on our mission to display the love of Jesus to everyone. Christ's call to love our enemies isn't just for their benefit; it's also for ours.

He wants us living in freedom; He doesn't want us bound up with the chains of bitterness or unkindness. In obedience to Him, we can find amazing joy, even in the midst of negativity and hostile circumstances. To obey Christ is to love Him and when we love Him, He releases the power that we need to love others. In this way, His love fulfills the greatest commandment in us, which is our ultimate mission here on earth (Matthew 22:36-39).

Compassionate Hearts

Recently on social media I read this quote by C.S. Lewis:

> *"To love at all is to be vulnerable. Love anything, and your heart will certainly be wrung and possibly broken. If you want to make sure of keeping it intact, you must give your heart to no one...lock it up safe in the casket or coffin of your selfishness. But in that casket—safe, dark, motionless, airless—it will change. It will not be broken; it will become unbreakable, impenetrable, irredeemable."*

We are confronted by our lack of goodness when we find ourselves faced with loving difficult people. It's a dilemma. The cowardly choice is to shun anyone who hurts you—cut them off and block them out. We might reason that, by doing so, we are protecting ourselves, but the reality is that self-preservation is spiritual suicide. Our hearts were never meant to be kept in safe chambers and caskets; they were created to love with wild abandon, just like God.

In his book *Wild at Heart*, author John Eldredge writes, *"Despite what you've been told, there is definitely something wild in the heart of*

God.'" [*] We see this truth in every sunrise and sunset. We see it in each motion of a roaring ocean wave or in a shooting star or a flickering flame. We see the vastness of God's wild underlying desires for every person walking this planet. There are dangerous risks in the wild, but there is also beauty there, too.

A hardened heart is a fearful heart and will not reflect Christ. It isn't strong. In fact, it's ineffectual and shatters easily. Compassion infuses our souls with sunshine! It melts away the bitterness from past hurt and compels us to love unlovable people. When Christ puts difficult people in your path, know that it is more about God's development of you than it is about your efforts to help the other person. God strategically plans every encounter for our growth and progression in Christ. He uses difficult people to mature us in His grace by expanding our capacity to exercise His word. He calls us to walk in the spirit and love them with His love. The enemy will place deterrents and obstacles in our way and discourage us from loving sacrificially. If he can trick us into believing that any unkindness from others is a personal attack and not a spiritual one, then he will stop at nothing to confuse us and distract us from being Jesus in our Judas situations. Remember, our fight is not against people (Ephesians 6:12); it's against *"spiritual forces of evil"* (ESV).

Throughout all the Gospels, we see Jesus loving everyone, including Judas. He embraced Judas. He included him, and he even trusted him with Kingdom information. The Lord entrusted His very life to His betrayer. Jesus knew from the beginning that Judas was appointed for disloyalty (John 6:70), but that did not deter Him from loving his traitor. In time, Jesus revealed Judas as "a devil" – indicating that He

---

* John Eldredge, *Wild at Heart: Discovering the Secret of a Man's Soul* (Nashville: Thomas Nelson, 2001), 32.

was aware of what was in the heart of this conniver, all along. Yet Christ never belittled him or casted him away. Christ had forgiveness for Judas, even before the betrayal. He loved Judas and shielded his identity from the other disciples throughout His entire ministry until the night appointed for Judas to fulfill the prophecy set before him (see Psalm 41:9 and John13:18).

Recently, I've been going through a difficult time in my personal life, so my sister-in-law invited me to a women's conference in Dallas, Texas. It was my first all-women's conference, and I was eager to go, as I desired to put some distance between myself and someone who had wounded me. I wanted the Lord to prepare my heart for His healing, so I arrived in Texas with great expectations!

With big hugs and giggles, Andrea and I headed to the conference where I was greeted with the opening topic: "Loving Those Who Don't Love You." (Ugggs and several eye rolls!)

"But I don't want to love mean girls," I whined to the Lord! To be completely honest, I was really hoping to hear a sermon more along the lines of, "Those who hurt you will reap the consequences! The Lord will avenge you and punish them all!" But, instead, I heard a profound message that reminded me of the love that marks a Christ-filled heart.

"Jesus kept the same posture of love even as He dealt with Judas," one of the speakers said. What a mind-blowing statement! Those words changed my life as they revealed how much my heart lacks the ability to operate in perfect love. (Lord, help my heart to love the way you do!)

Love is the evidence that Christ lives within! Our Savior has compassion for people right where they are. His love is constant from person to person and from circumstance to circumstance. He loved the crowd that shouted "Hosanna!" the same way He loved the crowd that cried, "Crucify Him!" He confronted those in the Sanhedrin who opposed the Father, yet humbled Him-self to dine with them. With honesty, He called the religious leaders, "vipers and snakes." But He never took offense when people attacked His character or identity. He knew who He was, and He invited others to know Him and experience His love.

There is beauty in rejection when it puts us in positions to love like Christ. Jesus demonstrated mercy over judgment as it says in James 2:13. He exemplified compassion for the sinner and the saint. Our Lord sympathized with those who did not treat Him with kindness or respect. Even now, He pleads with the world today, *"how often I have longed to gather you together, as a hen gathers her chicks under her wings, but you were not willing"* (Luke 34:13 NIV).

Jesus Christ longs to love those who simply have no regard for Him. He isn't delusional or in denial. He is well aware of the innermost of each one of us—secret intents, foul attitudes and the cynicism some people have toward Him. But each day with every sunrise, He extends His invitation of love and intimacy with God to all people. He doesn't hold grudges or take offense. He isn't indignant against unkindness in others. He willingly offers Himself to the world, knowing that some won't receive Him or appreciate Him. He calls us to have the same heart.

Colossians 3:12-15 states, *"Put on then, as God's chosen ones, holy and beloved, compassionate hearts, kindness, humility, meekness, and patience, bearing with one another.... And above all these put on love, which binds everything together in perfect harmony. And let the peace of Christ rule in your hearts."*

In this scripture, Paul calls us to acquire a Christ-like heart and attitude of compassion, kindness, humility, meekness, and patience. These virtues challenge us because they require us to deny ourselves. Thus, as we learn to love like Jesus, we have to become mature enough to recognize that not everyone will love us back. We are called by God to wear compassionate hearts, with no strings attached. There are no guarantees to what will result of that command. Naturally, we will find ourselves asking, "When is enough, enough?" As I write to you, I am battling these exact same questions in my own heart. Yet, I know that I cannot withhold my love from anyone if my goal is to please Jesus. I'm not saying it's easy. Lord knows I'm not saying it's easy! But odds are, we aren't living this Christian life because it's easy, are we? Loving like Christ can be a daily struggle in so many areas. It is a constant battle against our own self-interests and personal feelings. So, we must allow the power of God's Holy Spirit to take over our hearts and mold His compassion within us.

Where There are People, There are Problems

The year I was married, I lost a sweet friend. We celebrated my wedding together, and only months later our friendship unraveled. I often look at our picture, which hangs on my wall: we have big smiles in our wedding attire! I thought our friendship would last forever. I honestly believed our disagreement would eventually blow over, and we would move past it. But misunderstanding and high emotions prevented us from seeing each other's point of view. It got to the point where neither of us could understand the other anymore. In the last conversation we had, I told her that I loved her and that I would always be her friend, but she was unable to accept this as truth. After many attempts to salvage the relationship, I had to make the difficult choice to walk away.

Throughout my life, I've tried to create, maintain, and re-create relationships that just didn't have the mojo to withstand. I have had family members who didn't treat me the way I tried to treat them and I've known the sting of rumors and office gossip. I've been mistreated as much in church as well as in dorm rooms. Like you, I have shed my fair share of tears in the middle of the night. We've all known the pain of having a potential relationship fall apart. Some of you have called off engagements or endured divorce. Some of us work in hostile environments or find ourselves in the middle of family feuds. None of us have been without heartache, and each of us have been both the victim and the villain when it comes to hurt.

"Where there are people, there are problems," my dad has told me my whole life. The older I get, the more I recite this truth in my mind. In the face of negativity, we can stand our ground, in love, knowing that there is a spirit behind everything; those who we find difficult aren't always acting on their own. People are unkind for all sorts of reasons. A person's experience shapes the way they view the world and their actions are a reflection of what is in their hearts. Sometimes, people react in broken ways because they are broken inside. Insecurities can be vicious character flaws. Envious hearts produce toxic behaviors. So understand that unkind people have unhealthy views of themselves, which is why they have an unhealthy view of you—they have inadequate perceptions of who you are, so their behavior is based off of misinformation. When they see your confidence and blessings in the Lord, they may feel intimidated or jealous around you because they don't know how to access it for themselves. God's presence can be uncomfortable to those who are not following Him, so perhaps they reject you, not realizing they are really rejecting Him. Sometimes, it's not about you at all. Sometimes people just plain won't like you, for no logical reason. Jesus understands. In the book of John, He tells the disciples, "*They hated me without reason*" (John 15: 25 NLT).

So, I want to remind you, "nothing is personal; everything is spiritual." My mother says this so often, it's like a tattoo on my heart. Once we recognize this truth, we can readily operate in love and compassion towards difficult people. A heart filled with compassion isn't put off by problematic superficiality from others. Compassion is not possible without genuine kindness, and the kindness of Christ can put us in vulnerable places. Such vulnerability requires humility and meekness. It's humbling to put someone else's feelings above your own. It's meek to yield. I, for one, hate to yield. I hate to feel as if I am being stepped on or disregarded. Yet scripture demands that I lay my life down because that is what Christ did and continues to do. I know that if I am to be like Him, then I must love like Him, as well.

Listen, "*If the world hates you, know that it has hated me first*" (John 15:18 ESV). It's true: hostility arises in the spiritual realm when we begin to walk with the Lord. People we once considered friends may turn against us and those who once enjoyed having negative influences over us might begin to resent us once we start standing up for what is right. 1 Peter 4:4-5 declares, "*Of course, your former friends are surprised when you no longer plunge into the flood of wild and destructive things they do. So they slander you. But remember that they will have to face God, who will judge everyone, both the living and the dead*" (NLT).

Relationships can be messy and a break up, in any capacity, is quite difficult to endure. We who profess Christ do so at the risk of being rejected, not just from strangers, but even people that we care about. Realize that this is the situation that Jesus finds Himself in every day. He longs for His creation to love Him and want Him, but

He is often rejected, dismissed, and devalued by the very people He came to save. As we put on the identity of Christ, we mustn't be caught off guard when people dislike us or what we stand for. This is simply due to a lack of wisdom and spiritual perspective on their part—they don't understand Christ in us and their lack of understanding causes them to behave in opposition. Maturity in our faith will prevent us from becoming discouraged by the cost to love like Christ. We can have compassion for others, just as the Lord had compassion for us. Salvation is the only way to experience God's love, so know that those who don't have a relationship with God aren't able to operate in His love. Their drama and their problems should be met with our prayers, not our punishment.

Our flesh will always want to be avenged. It will always insist on being vindicated because our flesh is selfish and has no compassion. So, remember this—our right to be respected does not disqualify our responsibility to be kind. Under no circumstances should a child of God seek ways to hurt, belittle or embarrass others, no matter what they've done to you. That's not Christ and there is no glory where there is no Jesus! So, when you feel the urge to be justified, seek the Lord for a dose of His compassion. Instead of asking God to make things easier or give you an "out" from loving difficult people, start praying for more opportunities to share His perfect love. Ask the Lord to give you a heart filled with wisdom to separate people from their problems by loving them, in spite of the pain they cause. Through His Holy Spirit, we find the strength to love impossible people in incredible ways!

Even in the hurt from rejection, the disappointment, and the confusion, God is there, and He sees each tear. Yes, it feels so unfair, but God is in control. You aren't a victim, you are victorious and you *can* love those who don't love you, in Jesus' name! As we focus on loving with His grace, we will find ourselves operating with His heart toward those who don't realize how much they need Him. Our Heavenly Father will be quite pleased and one day we will hear Him say, "Well done." So, as we sojourn on and make it our hearts' desire to look like Jesus, love like Jesus, and live like Jesus, we must be prepared to be treated like Jesus, as well.

Pearls and Dust

When I became a Christian, I was so excited to tell my college friends! I shared with them how excited I was to really live for Jesus and how I would begin praying for them. They met my enthusiasm with stares and awkward smiles. The more I passed up on parties, and the more I began to voice my new opinions and faith, the more cynical they became. It all escalated one night in text message explosions. They didn't like my new life. They couldn't understand what God was doing, and I made the mistake of insistently trying to urge them to change along with me.

I discovered from this situation that the more I try to convince those unwilling to listen, the angrier they become. Passion is a good thing. And though the love we have for Christ and for others produces passion within our hearts, we can't impose our excitement on people who don't want it. My mother always says, "The Lord is a gentleman, and He never forces His love on anyone." We can't force relationships. We can't push our love. People will accept you or reject you. Either way, it's out of your control. We must learn how to let go, release those situations to the Lord, and move on. Jesus talked about this in His scenario of pearls and pigs: *"Do not give dogs what is sacred; do not throw your pearls to pigs. If you do, they may trample them under their feet, and turn and tear you to pieces"* (Matthew 7:6 NIV).

Our lives and our hearts are God's treasures. Our love and our sincerity are highly esteemed by our Heavenly Father. We were not created to be doormats or punching bags. We were created to be salt and light. Our kindness is a reflection of Christ within us. People will take advantage of our gentleness—we already know this— but this isn't an excuse to withhold our love, for any reason. Rather, we need to ask for wisdom to determine when to extend it and discernment to know when to move on. In my life, I have made the unfortunate mistake of thinking that my toleration of unkindness was love. I thought being lenient towards mistreatment was Christ-like and I have incorrectly accepted personal attacks of cruelty as signs that I wasn't loving hard enough. I have apologized for things I've never done, and in the attempt to be kind, I've kept quiet in moments when I should have spoken up. But such behavior is quite unhealthy.

"Trina, not everything is your fault," my friend BeBe often reminds me. "You need to tell the truth. Don't give people permission to run over you." I want to say the same to all of you. Christ treasures you, so *you* need to treasure *you*! Your love and your light are valuable and not meant for cruel mistreatment. Some people feel empowered by belittling others. But it's not wise to cower in passivity hoping things will smooth over. It's frustrating to face unjust ridicule and false criticism, but wisdom from God can help us filter the lies swarming around us in the dust of unkindness. Knowing when to move on, when to say "no," and how to set those important boundaries around what we will and will not tolerate will keep our hearts healthy and free to love, authentically, without hindrance.

In the Bible, we see Jesus setting healthy boundaries all the time! Throughout scripture, Jesus purposefully positioned Himself among people. In the crowds that followed Him, Jesus encountered the critics, the cynics, the devout, and those who were just spectators. He dealt with worthless arguments, unbelief from unbelievers, hostility and manipulation from agitated individuals and He dealt with positive and negative situations with wisdom.

Boundaries were important to Him; He stood by each word He spoke and did not cower in the face of hostility. Christ said "no" to inappropriate behaviors, like when the crowd tried to throw Him off the side of a cliff in Luke 4:28-30. He unapologetically shunned the devil and his temptations (Luke 4:1-13). He refused to be manipulated and used for selfish gain, as recorded in Matthew 16:23 and He boldly spoke the truth in love, even at the cost of upsetting people's feelings. Scripture also reveals that Jesus took personal time away from His friends for God in Matthew 6:6. He did all these things to maintain healthy boundaries for Himself and others.

Too many of us allow our lives to be polluted by mess when we fail to set up healthy boundary lines. We give our pearls to people who don't value them and we get lost in the dust that accumulates when we interact with unkind people and their behaviors. Christ knew His value. He knew who He was. He operated knowing the significance of His mission, regardless of the pressures and unkindness people placed on Him. It's just as appropriate for us to do the same, because we are who Christ says we are. We've been given a new and sacred heart filled with Kingdom treasures more valuable than pearls or rubies (Proverbs 3:15). Setting boundaries and standards are imperative to our ability to love like Jesus. Realize that putting standards in place doesn't reject people; it prevents problems. Guarding our hearts is a Biblical principal that we each must learn to exercise (Proverbs 4:23). We cannot love to our full potential if we are unwilling to tell the truth. "No" is sometimes the most honest and loving thing we can say to someone. "Yes" doesn't always produce positive results. Our abilities to set boundaries will guard our hearts against unnecessary drama. This is imperative to loving well!

Over the last few years, I have learned quite a bit about guarding my heart. I'm naturally an "open the flood gates" type of person. I'm all in, every time, with everyone and in everything; but this has caused me tremendous hurt in the past, due to a lack of discernment and the absence of boundaries. In one particular situation, excitement to connect and establish a friendship in my extended family motivated me to reach out in some extreme ways. I thought I had something beautiful to offer. I wanted to be a confidant and an encourager, so I would call to check up—thinking I was showing care and concern. But the responses were distant, so I would extend other invitations to persuade this person to get to know me. I tried to include her with my friends and offer my ideas to make her feel more involved. I gave my advice when I thought it was needed and I would send her morning scriptures to brighten her day. Over the span of several years, I extended lunch invitations that remained unaccepted and I endured several disappointments from intentional rejection. In spite of my efforts, the gap between us grew larger and my attempts at friendship resulted in mutual frustration. Out of enthusiasm, I had not set any boundaries. Her rejection was consistent, but I thought I could change her mind. I should have let the relationship go. I felt I was failing to be God's light in her life. I thought her reaction was a result of my failure. I wasn't sure what I had done wrong to offend, and I wasn't sure what to do to fix the situation. Why wouldn't she receive my friendship? Why was there so much disrespect and hostility towards me? I kept trying and calling and offering invitations... "Don't grow weary in well doing," I told myself. I presented my pearls in hopes of a changed response. It was exhausting!

Five years later and at the end of my patience, I laid it all at the Lord's feet in prayer.

"Jesus, You put this person in my life, but all my efforts have only pushed her further away from You and from me. Please show me what I can do to show her that my friendship is sincere."

And as I was crying, as I so often do, the Holy Spirit gently showed me that if my attempts at kindness were aggravating the person I was trying to reach, it wasn't really kind to keep reaching out. Not everyone we meet is meant to share in our destiny. Not everyone in our life, even in our families, has a place in our story or a part to play in our callings. Sometimes, our job is merely to love from afar and to give grace and space.

In this situation, my mistake was trying to prove myself, instead of accepting the person's disinterest in who I was and what I had to offer. I genuinely thought I was being encouraging and loving, but I was guilty of pouring too much water on a seed that had no interest in taking root. I realize, now, that my role in her life is to simply love her. That's really all that we can ever do. Loving doesn't mean tolerating unkindness, but it does mean to hope for the best by giving our best and trusting the Lord to take care of situations we cannot. So we can walk away, in love, by trusting Jesus to heal their hearts and ours, and be available should they ever need us. Yes, there are times when distance is necessary, because there are times when God asks us to draw a line and leave some circumstances in His hands. Jesus said, *"When you enter a house, stay there until you leave that town. If anyone will not welcome you or listen to you, shake the dust off your feet when you leave that place, as a testimony against them"* (Mark 6:10-11 NIV).

Learning how to love is key, but learning when to walk away in love is essential; sometimes, it's the most gracious thing to do. Quitting doesn't mean you're a quitter. You can still love from afar! It's important to learn how to handle opposition with respect and grace and not force or excessive zeal. Setting boundaries allows you to walk away from rejection by repositioning you to walk into circumstances of acceptance and destiny. Insisting on staying where you are not welcome can prove an intrusion on the person whom you hope to help. Eventually, such an imposition will harden their heart even more and leave you unnecessarily wounded in the aftermath. Know that God will take care of all things, so continue to love, even if it means from afar—being sure that you cover your opposers in prayer and seek God on how to love them in more effective ways. Nothing and no one is ever a lost cause. God is still at work, in each of us, so we don't need to worry and we don't need to become discouraged. We can face anyone and any circumstance with dignity, even in the midst of hostility, but we also must be sure to guard our hearts, in the process. So, stop throwing your pearls to people who insist on not wanting them. Shake off their dust and leave it all in God's hands.

Hope is a Treasure

Two weeks after my wedding, my friend Ashley joined me for my morning devotion. She came back the next day with Jessica and a week later, Kourtney joined as well. This was the beginning of Pearls of Hope Outreach. Within a month, there were nine girls coming to my house every week. Beth Moore and Kay Arthur were the authors we gleaned from; we were so excited to go deeper in God's Word together. By the end of the summer of 2013, word was out about our Bible studies, but not everyone was pleased. Some church officials in our city didn't want us to conduct Bible studies without their permission. I was even called into a meeting with a church leader who told me to stop the Bible studies immediately. Of course, the first person I called was my dad. He told me that people often distrust what they do not control. The leaders of that particular church feared we would contradict what they were teaching. The accusations from trusted mentors were alarming and unsettling. We could have crumbled in the wake of attack, but our desire for Bible study and fellowship lifted us above their dust and we continued meeting at my house every Tuesday. We are now in our fifth year of outreach. We've completed sixteen Bible studies together, and we are now a federally recognized non-profit organization! We had to choose to shake off the dust. If we hadn't, we would have missed out on our destinies for friendship, growth and impact! I would never have met Ariel or re-kindled my friendships with Sara, Amanda M., and Brandi-Joy. I would never have met Calena, Kita, Lydia, Keisha, Angela, or Brittany. And I wouldn't have had the opportunity to build more meaningful friendships with BeBe, Brandi Baker, Kourtney or Jessica Gray. We would never have gone to Honduras on a mission trip or been featured in a magazine or sold out Fashion Beyond Borders, which is our city-wide charity fashion show! There are so many ministries and people we would have never had the privilege of connecting with and learning from. Ashley and I would have never realized so many ideas and dreams together. I would never have discovered so many hidden talents and desires or seen God move in so many indescribable ways. Pearls of Hope Outreach could have been covered up in the dust of unkindness, but I'm so thankful that God displaced offense and replaced it with a hope and determination to simply move forward.

2 Corinthians 4:16-18 states, " *So we do not lose heart. Though our*

outer self is wasting away, our inner self is being renewed day by day. For this light momentary affliction is preparing for us an eternal weight of glory beyond all comparison, as we look not to the things that are seen but to the things that are unseen. For the things that are seen are transient, but the things that are unseen are eternal" (NIV).

Hope produces a platform for us to stand on in the midst of trying circumstances and negativity. Offense can knock us off our confidence, but our hope in Christ will sustain us, through it all. That's why I love the name of our organization, Pearls of Hope Outreach, because hope is a treasure. Though not everyone will treasure your treasures, God continuously does. Our love is more priceless than pearls and the hope that God has implanted within each of our hearts will sustain us as we keep about our Father's business. The dust of offense can dull even the brightest jewel and opposition can make the way unbearable at times, but we should always maintain hearts that are happy to love everyone—friends and enemies alike. We must be willing to love whomever we come across, but we must also be cautious not to force on others the treasures God has entrusted to us. Not everyone will value them. We cannot afford to hold ourselves hostage to hostile circumstances. The joy of the Lord is our strength (Nehemiah 8:10) and our hope must always rest in Him!

"I know you want to do the Christian thing, Katrina," my friend Kourtney, told me. "It might feel like you've run out of cheeks to turn, but you can do it!" I want to say the same to you. You can do it! I know in the thick of it all, it's easier said than done. To be honest, I, too, am weak in this area. I am super-dramatic: I cry when I'm happy, and I cry when I am sad and pissed off. I tend to filter my entire experience by what has moved me the most. More times than what's appropriate, I've allowed the negative and hurtful circumstances in my life to cloud my vision of the wonders that God is creating all around me. It's time for us all to stop doing this. It's time for us to stand on the hope of God's promises and stop throwing away our pearls. Hope is our treasure and it is our confidence that what God is doing will be completed. No one can alter His plans for you. No one can displace His promises in your life. No matter what they say, or how they treat you, you are an overcomer, in Jesus name! The unkindness in this world is a result of sin. Those who are unkind operate from a wounded and broken place, due to a lack of Christ's healing in their hearts. Don't let broken people break you.

Listen ladies, we can't allow ourselves to become so focused on the rejections and the opposition we face from others that we forget God's promise to uphold us and to be our shield in the midst of those who seek to overtake us.

> *"You, O Lord, are a shield all around me. You are my glory and the lifter of my head"*, Psalm 3:3 (NIV).

There are no circumstances where you are defeated. There is no person who can block you from God's calling over your life. It's not our job to prove ourselves, it's our responsibility to maintain hope by loving those God has entrusted us to love, while trusting Him with the outcome. Our kindness is not passivity. Our hope is never displaced when anchored in Jesus. Never lose sight of this truth. Jesus came to love people back to the Father, through the hope and gift of salvation. What is happening in your life now is only preparing you for a higher capacity to love like Christ. This is our mission and hope of glory! So let's all practice the grace of "letting go" and walking away: from our hurts, our anger, our resentment and our pain. Seek the Holy Spirit about when to speak and when to stay silent. Don't feed strife. It only produces more of itself. Pray for more love and hope in all situations. Learn to be a peacemaker and a giver of grace. Value your treasures, and treasure the valuables of others. Know that God will guide you through these many shadows. Our hearts are in His right hand, and our lives are vibrantly strung like pearls for His Kingdom. Our hope is in Him, so we have nothing to lose or prove.

Grace, Please

A few weeks ago, I encountered a surprise house call. The phone call caught me off guard and I was scrambling to give an answer to the visit request. Now let me paint this picture for you: I was in my underwear, as I had just washed my hair. I was going through my tedious detangling process, and my curls were like a matted bird's nest! The kitchen looked atrocious. I had been boiling spaghetti while doing my hair in the other room, and out of laziness, chose not to put the top on the pot of sauce. Red splatters had spewed everywhere, leaving lava colored marks on the stovetop and floor. Dripping mascara left stains around my eyes from the shower, and my knees were ashy! Though the last thing I wanted to do was oblige an unexpected visit, out of politeness, I agreed.

Oblivious to the fact that the visit was an intrusion, my visitor explained that she would be arriving in five minutes. That's not a lot of time to turn a catastrophe into the pristine abode that I pride myself in presenting to company. As I pulled my hair in a bun, I frantically wiped the floor with a rag under my feet while continuing the conversation. I told her that once Jarrett, my husband, came home, she was welcome to stay for dinner as well.

"Jarrett's not home yet?" she asked.

"No, it's just me right now. He's still at work," I answered.

"You're home by yourself? Where's the baby?" she questioned. "Well, my mom has her for the afternoon today," I replied. A silence fell. "Oh," she said, "I think today wouldn't really be good after all. I just remembered an errand I probably need to run, and I don't think I'll have time to do it tomorrow. I'm sorry, I won't be able to come by today."

I was stunned. All the white noise in the room came to the forefront and I felt deaf from the ringing of disrespect in my ears. But even as the hurt swelled up in my throat and hot tears puddled in my eyes, I had to consider the person and not the action. This person was not intentionally disrespectful; she was just too distracted by her own agenda and although I felt insulted, I told her that I understood and I would see her another time. There was no point in discussing how she had hurt my feelings because that might have produced an even bigger conflict or misunderstanding. So, I chose to let it go and give grace by showing love instead of defending myself. After we hung up, I flung my phone onto the couch with all my might and took another shower.

Offense is easily felt when we sense personal disrespect or inconsideration, but Christ in us compels us to show grace in those moments of insult and disregard. Grace is desperately necessary in everyday life. People will believe the sincerity of your love by your willingness to shake off the dust of their offense. I use the word willingness and not ability, because in ourselves we aren't able. We each come to a point where we just don't have any more cheeks to turn! So we must rely on God's grace to produce beauty when we feel offended.

The Lord keeps teaching me personal lessons in giving grace, over and over again. I've been disappointed by people I've trusted and stung from feeling unprotected and undefended. I've been blamed for things

I haven't done and been called stuck up and judgmental by people who never cared enough to get to know me. I've blindly walked into situations unaware that they would end in catastrophe, and I know the embarrassment of being bullied in public, even as an adult. You have your own versions of similar stories. Some of you have gone through so much worse, but Christ commands that we love, regardless. This is His highest calling for us all.

Greatness is produced through the trials of life. Some issues in our lives are strategically placed to humble and mature us and position us into our highest calling. A pearl is made from acid. A coal that suffers no pressure will never become a diamond. Every rose has thorns to teach us that the heartache of life builds great beauty! We can find strength in God's love through the giving of grace. What is happening now is only preparing you for the greatness ahead. We won't experience God's comforting presence unless we are uncomfortable. We won't experience His power until we are weak. God's grace is magnified when we are lacking and His healing occurs when we are suffering. The Apostle Paul spoke about an irritant that he suffered. He called it his "thorn in the flesh." In 2 Corinthians 12:7-10 Paul wrote, *"I was given a thorn in my flesh... three times I pleaded with the LORD to take it away from me. But he said to me, "My grace is sufficient for you, for my power is made perfect in weakness." ...That is why, for Christ's sake, I delight in weaknesses, in insults, in hardships, in persecutions, in difficulties. For when I am weak, then I am strong"* (NIV).

A thorn might be in our flesh, but it need not be in our spirits. God's grace is sufficient! We, who are in Christ, must give grace generously because this reflects the heart of Heaven. Grace reveals the nature of God who removes offenses and pardons guilt and sin. Since Christ resides within us, there is no excuse for willingly allowing unforgiveness to fester in our hearts. We mustn't allow our spirit to take on the position of those who have offended us. Victory is ours in Jesus over every stronghold and any attack. Offenses build up fences. The only purpose of a fence is to lock you in and lock you out: out of your calling, out of your destiny, out of your sincerity and out of your effectiveness. The only way to prevent a fence, or rather an offense, is to take any negative thoughts captive and cast them down (2 Corinthians 10).

This is a lesson as much for me as it is for you. I'm bad about replaying scenarios in my mind. It's a terrible thing to do, because it builds up negativity and anxiety. There is power in your thoughts as well as in your words. Break through the lock and stronghold of unforgiveness using the weapons of 2 Corinthians 10:3-5, *"For though we live in the world, we do not wage war as the world does. The weapons we fight with are not the weapons of the world. On the contrary, they have divine power to demolish strongholds. We demolish arguments and every pretension that sets itself up against the knowledge of God, and we take captive every thought to make it obedient to Christ"* (NIV).

In my life, I have strained my heart with afterthoughts and regrets of how I might have done or said things differently to salvage relationships and misunderstandings. I have even warred within my heart and mind over "come backs" I wish I had have been quick enough to use in the moment, in order to defend myself from cruel words and mean girls. But I am learning that beating one's self up and doing penance for the past doesn't correct the present circumstances. In other words, if it didn't happen, it's counterproductive and unspiritual to waste time wishing that things were different. There are choices that can only be redeemed by God, and there are regrets that will only find a remedy as the Lord converts all things for our good. Only through His love can we ever move forward from hurts of the past. When we replay painful memories or hold onto hurt feelings from unkindness or rejection, our flesh wins and the enemy gains invitation to stir more strife. We have to put our flesh to death and place our pride to the side as we draw on grace to love our brothers and sisters in sincerity, through forgiveness. Sometimes, this even requires that we forgive ourselves.

God's grace says, "Let it go." He reminds me, sometimes daily, "Katrina, let it go." I invite you to write your name here: "____, let it go!"

Recognize that what is in a person's heart will come out of them. People are unkind because their hearts aren't whole. They lash out at you as a result of their own brokenness and insecurities. A chipped diamond will cut you. Handle such people with caution, and ask the Lord to soften those edges, as only He can. You don't have the tools to change hearts. All you can do is offer the best of Christ's love in every situation. There are circumstances that will never get a second chance and there are people and places that we will never be able to revisit, so give them and your-self some grace, please.

"Fix your thoughts on what is true and good and right. Think about things that are pure and lovely, and dwell on the fine, good things in others. Think about all you can praise God for and be glad about it", Philippians 4:8 states (TLB). We can steer the attitudes of our heart by what we think in our minds. So when we release words of blessing, prosperity, safety, and salvation over those who have wronged us, walls that went up in offense are knocked down by grace; maybe not in their hearts, but definitely in ours! God's love and compassion can then flow inwardly for our healing and outwardly for theirs. That's what God's grace is all about- reaching into places where we cannot!

The truth is, in all love there is heartache and sacrifice, both of which makes the giving of grace difficult, yet very necessary. We must exhibit the grace we have been given in spite of our feelings or circumstances. No love is bullet proof, and butterflies don't last forever. Our love must consist of more than feelings and flattering words. Remember, grace isn't distributed to cover up problems. Instead, we bring every situation to a problem-solving God. We are each in need of daily doses of grace. To whom much is given much is required (Luke 12:48). As Christ has given us much, so we give to others.

"Grace is giving what you need the most to someone who needs it more, but deserves it less". This is a quote from a minister at my brother's church. I wrote this in my Bible as a truthful reminder. God loves people who don't deserve it. His love is for transgressors—those who have made mistakes and need His goodness. Aren't we the best examples of this?

God's kindness leads us to His grace. I can't explain it, but there is so much freedom when we trust God with our thorns. He will pluck out, prune and cut anything that hinders the flow of His love through us (John 15:2). God's strength is made perfect in our weakness and brokenness. We will sometimes find ourselves in seasons of mistreatment and offenses, but He is still faithful. He is still good. There is beauty to be found in our moments of rejection and in the face of unkindness because God is with us. Beauty follows His footsteps, and He has promised to never leave us. God is within us! His grace is abundant and we can trust His heart and His intentions for us. All things work together for the good of those who love Him and underneath it all, He is creating us to be His treasures, His diamonds, and His string of pearls for the world to see!

Freedom in Forgiveness

An ability to love in every capacity is foreign to us. But through the power of God's Holy Spirit, as we learn to love imperfect people, Christ's perfection is unveiled. We die to our natural feelings, our pride, our self-righteousness, and our need to be justified so we can forgive. We must devote our hearts to God to let go of the demand to be respected and treated fairly. Our "good girl" ID cards don't obligate others to treat us kindly. Christ was not treated fairly, and neither will we always be.

Matthew 5:44-48 gives us Jesus' words:

> *"But I tell you, love your enemies and pray for those who persecute you, that you may be children of your Father in Heaven. He causes his sun to rise on the evil and the good, and sends rain on the righteous and the unrighteous. If you love those who love you, what reward will you get? Are not even [sinners] doing that? And if you greet only your own people, what are you doing more than others? Do not even pagans do that? Be perfect, therefore, as your Heavenly Father is perfect"* (NIV).

People will try to push you towards unkindness because they need a reason to support their hostility towards you. Don't give them one. Love from Christ's perfect love. Don't give into the pressure of petty vengeance. Women are particularly skilled in presenting a façade of strength through cattiness. TV is full of reality shows that applaud such behavior. These outside temples of physical beauty are often more immaculate than the inward soul. But, sooner or later, even the most beautiful sand castles crumble. I've seen it time and time again –mean girls who one day need a friend. You've seen it, too. Maybe it's even happened to you. Any seed sown will eventually produce fruit: either positive or negative. We need to be available when life hits hard against those who have wronged us. They will need a safe place to go. Quite possibly, God chose to connect them with you so you could help them in their time of need.

It's a difficult decision to love those who've hurt us. It's impossible without God's power. We need God's love and the strength of His Holy Spirit to operate in obedience in cases such as these. I can't love someone in the strength of Katrina because Katrina is flawed and imperfect. My fragile heart can break, and the edges of my brokenness can stab the very person I originally was trying to love. No, I cannot operate in my own strength to love or forgive difficult and unkind people. We all need the Holy Spirit's power to love consistently and graciously and He desires to perform this work in us. The miracle unveiling is that we don't have to operate from damaged emotions or anger over past hurts. The love of God is our shield. *"Let His banner over me be love,"* Song of Solomon 2:4 declares (NIV); we can choose to lean on Him so that our feelings don't overwhelm us.

If love is our greatest calling, as 1 Corinthians 13:13 states, then no other love should consume our hearts more than our love for Christ. He wants to be preeminent in all things—even in our difficulties. It's through His Spirit that we will learn how to extend the grace that He has bestowed on us. To love like Christ, we must first be in love with Christ. Once we realize that those who mistreat us are in bondage to their own unkindness, we begin to understand how great God's compassion was on us when we once rejected Him. Yet God still extended a great grace to us, as Romans 5:8 states, *"But God demonstrates His own love for us in this: While we were still sinners, Christ died for us."*

Forgiveness is not automatic, but it is possible. It's difficult to forgive when we know we're not at fault. But, when we feel wronged or attacked, if we don't immediately give the rejection and hurt to the Lord —meaning if we don't forgive—then roots of bitterness, resentment, and self-pity will surely begin to grow. Ladies, we must be so careful not to entertain offenses. Forgive quickly, and let things go, because resentment produces hatred. And hatred is out of the will of God for us. *"For if you forgive men their trespasses, your Heavenly Father will also forgive you. But if you don't forgive their trespasses, neither will your Father forgive yours,"* (Matthew 6:14-15 ESV). This is made possible only through God's love.

Extending love amidst our hurt seems unbearable, but in Christ, we are able! Forgiveness is possible only through the absence of pride and the presence of grace. It starts with our willingness and, in time, God will heal our wounds and expand our capacity to extend His love and forgiveness. So be careful to rid yourself of the dust that makes your life look dirty. Hurting people hurt other people. We know this. So we must love and pray and forgive to combat the pain that circulates in our world. No, we aren't perfect—we are not finished products. We are in process, and we all have many lessons to learn in this area. Hurtful experiences can knock us off course. But we've got to get up and shake off the dust by focusing our hope on Jesus. You'll fail in your calling if you are unable to love and forgive. We can't profess God's unconditional love while living as captives to our limited capacity to forgive others. We need a fresh saturation of God's love to empower us in our human weaknesses, so we can move past offenses and give grace beyond our hurts.

Forgiving and loving go hand and hand like eyeliner and mascara. They make the picture perfect and complete! Never forget God loves the person you can't stand. As daughters of God, we must operate in the perfect love of our Father by forgiving freely because we know we've been forgiven and set free by our good and gracious God! At times, it might be difficult, but we can love perfectly because we have Christ's perfect love residing within us. Not everyone will like you. I know...I know...you're an awesome person! You have a beautiful heart, and your intentions are pure. I know the urgency you feel. I have similar hopes for the difficult people in my life, as well. But when people are cruel, we must find our freedom in forgiveness. Nursing our hurts prevents healing, and hardening our hearts blocks blessings, so we must walk in forgiveness if we want to experience an abundant life in Christ. Since we need more of God to love God, then we most certainly need more of Him to love other people. As my friend Amanda Myers says, "I'm just needing more of Jesus today". And she's so serious! Are you serious about His love? Are you "just needing more of Jesus?" Because if you are, He will give you what you desire (Psalm 37:4).

Forgiveness is the ultimate act of love. If we are to be Christ's image-bearers, we must be lovers and forgivers just like Him! I am not perfected in this commandment yet. The past year has been one of deep growth and healing for me in this area. The Holy Spirit has been teaching me by correcting me and reminding me that Christ has forgiven me of more than what I sometimes struggle to forgive in others. Keeping that sort of mindset is humbling and makes me grateful that Christ's love for me isn't shaky the way my love can sometimes be towards others. Even now, as I encourage all of you to forgive, the Lord is encouraging me in the same area. He reminds me constantly that I have been called to love people, and to love them well. I'm not always successful. Sometimes I retreat from those who have wounded me, and it's my nature to avoid environments of unkindness. To be honest with you, I am still suffering from a broken heart over the friendship I tried so hard to develop within my extended family. It's been truly devastating to be told I'm not important or necessary in someone's life and that they liked their family better before I came along. Words like that pierce my soul and honestly, in the wake of my devastation and pain, I am struggling with anger and resentment. I desire freedom. Don't we all?

God assures us that we'll never regret loving and that our willingness to forgive others sets us free. He has expressed His love perfectly through Jesus and asks us to do the same. Others are not required to accept the love that we extend, yet we are still required, by Christ, to extend that love with a pure heart—this is true freedom. Operating in unforgiveness results from a lack of love and will never produce the presence of Christ. It's the enemy who lives in dissention and disharmony, but Christ empowers us to operate beyond our natural reactions of offense. The absence of love is the absence of God as God is love. 1 John 4:8 reveals, *"But if a person isn't loving and kind, it shows that he doesn't know God—for God is love"* (TLB). So let's love well! Even in our hurt, even in our anger, let Christ's love overcome it all! Though we may feel rejected at times, we are never forgotten. Christ sees us and He is with us, through it all. He desires to develop us into treasures, unspeakable, so allow yourself to go through the process of loving the unlovable and forgiving as Christ has forgiven you. You won't always be perfect, but you will begin to change more into a woman who harbors the heart of Christ. This is true beauty and freedom.

Questions for Discussion

1. Reflect on a time when you were challenged to love a difficult person. What was the situation? What was your initial reaction to their unkindness and what happened as a result of your love toward them? Did healing result or are you still being challenged to love?

2. Consider ways in which Christ can use your brokenness to reflect His beauty in your life. How can God use you to show His love when you're called to love an unlovely person?

3. Just as we receive grace from God, we must have a heart to share the same with others. Consider how you can be more gracious to a difficult person in your life. Reflect on ways that God has showered His grace upon you, and ask the Lord to help you in your dealings with offense and unkindness.

CHAPTER 9

A Journey with Jesus

When my daughter was born, I waited for the angelic choir to float down from Heaven and play their harps. I waited in expectation for the tingly feelings that everyone says you are supposed to experience the first time they take your naked, crying baby straight from your womb and put her on your chest. I remember looking down at this little girl—so calm and tranquil in my arms. I could barely fathom the significance that I had birthed a baby! The magnitude of the title, "mother", is the sweetest and most terrifying identity one could possess. From that moment, I knew my world would never be the same. But, to my surprise, the angelic choir never showed up. I waited and waited for Gabriel himself to come down out of Heaven, blow his trumpet, and give me the love sensation everyone says you're supposed to experience. It never happened. No cherubim or seraphim came to sing songs from Heaven. Tinker Bell did not blow pixie dust in my face to make me fly around in my room. Instead, I was in an oversized hospital gown, wearing big blue plastic panties, while I breastfed a little girl who had no idea her mommy had just undergone major surgery. I was tired, sore, and weak.

For those of you who are now pregnant, I will spare you the details of my labor story. But I will tell you this: it was nothing like the blogs described. I ended up having to have an emergency C-section and then a blood transfusion because I lost so much blood. My family and I stayed in the hospital for five days and I endured endless amounts of pain and confusion. Each morning, as I breastfed this little, tiny person, my hopes for some sort of spark of something extraordinary went unmet. She didn't even look like me, and those of you who know me know what a blow that was to my vanity! Still, she was cute, and she smelled good; but I didn't feel connected to her in any way.

During my recovery, one nurse asked me if my love thermometer was bursting. I just looked at her with a blank face. Deep down in my soul, the answer was, "no." The monumental wave of love that I'd read about in all the books didn't come true for me in the hospital. All of my family and friends gushed over us both. Everyone wanted to take pictures and hold the baby and kiss me. I was happy to have their support, but I couldn't understand why explosive love hadn't moved me to tears. I thought perhaps I had the "baby blues" i.e. postpartum depression. A friend of my brother's had shared with me her experience with this, but survey after survey confirmed this wasn't my case. I was happy and alert. And I was sociable and as energetic as possible for a woman recovering from having had her uterus sliced open. Breastfeeding was a breeze, and my daughter was very healthy. My brother and Andrea came down from Texas. My cousins and aunts came in from Ohio. My Pearls all came to visit me multiple times, and my parents and in-laws were very involved. My mother stayed with us for three weeks to help me transition. Jarrett, my darling husband, was a true champion for me. I felt loved all around, and I thanked God for these blessings.

So what was wrong with me? Nothing at all! What I began to realize was that my love for Kailyn wasn't instantaneous. It was more of a developmental relationship. With each passing day, as I nursed her, sang to her, kissed her face, and changed her diapers, my love for her grew more and more. Each stage of her life brought a new joy to mine. And one morning, several weeks later, I finally got that tingly chill down my spine. Right after her feeding, as I softly patted her back for a burp, her little lips brushed across my cheek and I felt that exhilaration only a mother experiences. It was sweeter than anything an angelic choir could have produced!

Kailyn is now two years old, and my heart is filled with an incredible longing to share my existence with her. She's so smart and sweet! She sings songs about Jesus and is obsessed with blueberries! She loves to pick flowers and play with chalk. Her laugh sounds like a million little bubbles all popping at once! With her big brown eyes and curly hair, she resembles my husband, yet definitely has my sensitive heart. As she grows, I find my love for her is growing deeper and stronger, as is her love for me. At the beginning, I was simply her source for life—her means to an end. Now she lives each day with a new understanding of who "mommy" is. I, too, am learning and growing with a new understanding of my identity and relationship with her. I share this story as a comparison to a relationship with Christ. Though it may start gradually with uncertainty at first, the goodness of God we encounter in each new day compels us to love Him more and more.

Growing in intimacy with God isn't merely a state of mind; it is a state of experiencing, exploring and developing with Him by simply receiving His love and surrendering our struggles to Him. Out of love for Jesus, we are compelled to live our lives for His glory, withholding nothing from pursuing His will. This is what makes our lives shine! Success in Christ and closeness to God is more than acknowledging His existence or doing a few nice things. The Christian's life is marked by a changed heart and life through faith in Christ. We trust that He'll activate and release His Spirit through us to produce good fruit and accomplish His plans in us. As we begin to desire more of Him, He invites us deeper into the experience of this love relationship. This is what separates us from "the good girls".

Scripture tells us that it is not our natural reaction to love and obey God (Romans 3:11). In fact, it's the exact opposite. Our flesh and sin nature desires more of itself. God is Spirit, so we must be taught to desire spiritual things. It does not come instantaneously; so don't be discouraged if you haven't experienced tangible feelings toward God. It's OK! You can breathe now! Accept this and move on because loving Jesus is a developmental journey. It's not based on feelings. It's a progression towards His perfection and this takes patience on our part and grace on His. There's no "Ta-Da!" moment. Yet, each day, with every experience and every obedience, we will grow closer to Him and become more like Him.

We will never attain perfection until we meet Him face to face (1 John 3:32). But as we focus on Him one day at a time, He begins a work of righteousness from the inside out, which transforms us beyond our feelings and personal aspirations. His life begins to take over and spills into everything we do and everything we are. How we treat others and ourselves changes as we journey on and grow closer to Christ. How we handle disappointment changes. How we endure the pressures of life changes. Even the way we date should be different, as we become Christ-focused women who want the Lord's best. No longer are we satisfied with momentary amusement or personal gains. Instead, we realize that we must love others in a Christ-like manner by putting their needs and best interests before ours.

In 1 John 4:19, The Bible says that we love God only because He loved us first. He loved us beyond who we were and offered His salvation as an investment in our eternity. He gave His life for us when we didn't even want the gift that He offered. He loved us when we did not love Him. Christ doesn't carelessly invite us into this love journey; in His word, God tells us to *"taste and see that the Lord is good"* (Psalm 34:8 ESV). He says to us, "Sample my love and see just how good your life in Christ can be!" To taste means to try Him out. He's asking us to give Him a chance to show us that He is everything He says He is. We don't need to trust Him blindly. Try Him out and determine if having a relationship with Him is worth it. He is confident that we will find that He is not simply a "higher power." He is God, and He is love. His character of goodness is guaranteed. God has a unique journey for each of us. He gives unique assignments and individualizes His promises. None of us will have the exact same experiences on our journey with Jesus. His Holy Spirit will move over each of us in different ways, producing different results and bestowing unique blessings. We will never experience such good things without Him. He is calling us all to take steps of faith but not in ourselves. It's in His love. Jesus invites us to live beyond our own attempts at being good. As we try God and His love, we will begin to see His goodness in our lives, gradually at first, then in multiplied ways as we venture on.

Signs and Wonders

Last summer, I had a conversation with a young lady who was making some terrible choices. I really had compassion for her because she was in a mess that I had familiarity with from my past mistakes. She kept saying, "Every night I ask God to give me a sign about what to do."

"But you already know what to do," I told her. "I want all of God's blessings for you, so just do what's right," I said.

"I know," she answered, "But I'm just waiting for God to show me a sign so that I'll know for sure."

God is always speaking. Just because we don't recognize it doesn't mean He is silent. He isn't silent. He speaks through His word. It's up to us to notice and hide His word in our hearts for future reference and obedience. Unfortunately, many of us aren't dedicating quality time in our Bibles, are we? We aren't searching the scriptures or positioning ourselves to hear the Lord through prayer and fasting. We allow too many distractions to steal time away from pressing into God's presence, and this hinders us from hearing His voice. But if we want closeness with Jesus, we've got to put in the time and dedication required to open up our spiritual ears and invite His presence. Microwave Christianity doesn't exist. If we're honest, many of us would rather listen to the results of someone else's quiet time than to actually make time for our own. So we default by insisting on collecting God's Word from other individuals who seem more capable than us, without examining this with scripture. We accept opinions that confuse us and hinder our growth. So, we ask for signs because we're not confident or secure. We search for proof because we aren't really sure what we believe.

John 6:28-30 presents us with the scene of a conversation Jesus had with religious men about signs and proof. *"Then they asked him, "What must we do to do the works God requires?" Jesus answered, "The work of God is this: to believe in the one He has sent." So they asked him,*

"What sign then will you give that we may see it and believe you? What will you do?" (NIV).

The religious people in Jesus' day spent their entire lives praying for the Savior of the world. But as they conversed with Him in living flesh, they kept requiring a sign and some proof. "Confirmation, confirmation," they demanded! They insisted, "Give us a word, a sign—a proof!" Their desire for proof hindered their willingness to believe. We know from Hebrews 11:6, *"And without faith it is impossible to please God, because anyone who comes to Him must believe that He exists and that He rewards those who earnestly seek Him"* (NIV). Jesus used scripture to confirm Himself. But they couldn't see it, because they simply didn't believe.

Ladies, we need to stop looking around for signs. Either we believe our Savior, or we don't. A journey with Jesus does not involve seeking out signs as proof of His love or validation of our salvation. It has become so usual in church culture to refuse to move until we have received a "word" of confirmation from another source. God so often places desires in our hearts or shares a truth in His still small voice, but instead of believing Him at His word and seeking the Holy Spirit through scripture, we go from sermon to sermon, book to book, or person to person, searching for some sort of outside confirmation. But God says in 1 Thessalonians 5:24, He will do all that He has promised.

Searching for proof from the words of others is not faith in Christ. It's faith in man. True, there are definitely times when God calls someone to speak words of encouragement that confirm what He has already placed in our hearts. We have been blessed to have leaders and teachers, mentors and friends who cover us and lift us up in prayer. Some of us have certainly been on the receiving end of miracles and answered prayers because of our leaders and their faithfulness. Thank God for them! They exemplify how to live lives for God's glory. But Christ encourages us to come boldly to the throne of grace for ourselves (see Hebrews 4:16). The same Holy Spirit that lives in our leaders also lives in you! God is producing Himself in each of us, according to His purpose. Spiritual confirmation and prophetic encouragement from other people only happens according to God's desires and no one else's. And it does not happen all the time. God's Spirit is not subject to our itinerary and schedule or the timing of a conference. He moves when He wants, as He wants, and for whom He wants. His Spirit moves for hearts that believe Him at His word, regardless of outside sources of confirmation.

While I was growing up, my mom would often say, "Salvation is so simple that most people miss it." How true this is! We complicate our walk with Christ by incorporating more than He has instructed. At times, we tend to put too much emphasis on *what* to do and *how* things will come about, instead of trusting God and His process. Many of us have jumped too soon and moved ahead of what God was doing. If we'll only believe His word, He will instruct us on the *what,* and reveal to us the *how.* It's not as complicated as we sometimes try to make it. All God asks us to do is accept His gift of salvation, believe His truth, and obey His word. Accept. Believe. Obey. How simple! As we begin to live out this salvation in its truest form, we discover God's presence and His word are not subject to His miracles. God is good whether He moves or not. However, He does move greatly in each of our lives and sometimes, He even chooses us to be part of the miracles He performs. He is the one in control and His plans will be fulfilled in His timing and in His way. We can trust Him to lead us by His Spirit; we do not need to be led by signs.

If we're honest, navigating this life by ourselves is overwhelming.

But that is why Christ sent the Comforter—the Holy Spirit. As Pastor Thomas in Greensboro says, "We have a navigation system living on the inside of us." We have the working of the Holy Spirit to guide us. John 16:13 states, *"But when He, the Spirit of truth, comes, He will guide you into all the truth. He will not speak on His own; He will speak only what He hears, and He will tell you what is yet to come"* (NIV).

The Holy Spirit is our confirmation! He leads and guides us, and His leading is only made clear and confirmed through the Word that we should be storing within our hearts. In our natural selves, we won't have any energy if we don't eat food. In a like manner, we can't expect to hear God's voice if we're not putting His word in our hearts. A sermon once a week is not going to fill our spirits up to withstand the pressures of this world. And our favorite song, although uplifting and encouraging, won't produce the quality of growth that we need to pass our day to day tests. Reading our Bibles and praying God's Word equips us and brings spiritual growth, stamina and the confirmations we seek in order to make God-pleasing decisions in our various circumstances and situations. The Spirit confirms what we read in scripture because every word is true. 2 Timothy 3:16 is the assurance we need: *"All Scripture is God-breathed and is useful for teaching, rebuking, correcting and training in righteousness, so that the servant of God may be thoroughly equipped for every good work"* (NIV).

"Blessed assurance, Jesus is mine!" He alone is our proof! We don't need any signs or wonders outside of Him. "Be careful. We can be enslaved to our desires to be assured and miss out on receiving the fruits of simply operating in obedience and faithfulness," Loran Livingston, my pastor in Charlotte, NC, has said in past sermons. Our obedience prepares us for blessings. God's faithfulness develops His righteousness in us. Regardless of where we place our trust or what we believe, God will carry out His plans. We aren't the only vessels He can use. He chooses the faithful ones who will trust Him at His word. Jesus said to the disciple, Thomas, *"Because you have seen, you believe, but blessed are those who have not seen, but still believe"* (John 20:29 NIV).

There is a blessing in believing, and believing comes from hearing the Word of the Lord (Romans 10:17). I wonder if our obsession with signs is actually a reflection of our lack of knowing scripture? We can't believe what we don't know. We can't have faith in things of which we are unaware. It is in scripture that we find the heart of God and learn to discern His voice and leading. God is always speaking, but are we listening? Are we reading the Bible? Are we designating time for the Lord? Keep in mind the purpose of scripture is edification and not education. Our desire for Scripture shouldn't be based on obligation or guilt or carnal curiosity. The Bible is much more than a self-help book. We all should be moved in our very souls to spend more time with Jesus. We must begin to invite God's Spirit to develop a hunger in us for His word because without God's presence, we will never be whole.

Consider the story of Caleb and Joshua. These were two young men who showed great faith in God. They found themselves among men who were too afraid to secure the promised land. These men tried to discourage the people, as Numbers 13: 27-33 records, but Caleb and Joshua held a different attitude than the others. Verse 30 states, *"Then Caleb silenced the people before Moses and said, 'We should go up and take possession of the land, for we can certainly do it"* (NIV). Joshua then said, in Numbers 14:6-9, *"If the Lord is pleased with us, he will lead us into that land, a land flowing with milk and honey, and will give it to us... do not be afraid of the people of the land, because we will devour them. Their protection is gone, but the Lord is with us. Do not be afraid of them*" (NIV).

Caleb and Joshua believed the word of the Lord and declared it without shame. God's response to their trust and faithfulness was, "*Because my servant Caleb has a different spirit and follows me wholeheartedly, I will bring him into the land, and his descendants will inherit it*" (Numbers 14:24 NIV). Joshua and Caleb didn't require anything more than God's word. How differently our lives and our faith would look if we followed suit? Our cravings for proof only prove that there is still uncertainty in our hearts. When we demand proof from God to confirm our choice to obey, we could be in jeopardy of dishonoring the God we hope to serve. Signs don't produce relationship. They are religious and have no real power. A superstitious mind requires proof; a heart who trusts in Christ says, "I believe you, Lord."

Scripture tells us over and over again that God can be trusted. But do we trust Him or do we just hope that He can be trusted? There really is a difference. I invite us to explore our hearts in this matter as we sojourn on in our journey with Jesus. Horoscopes are not appropriate reading material for Believers. Religious artifacts made by human beings won't get us any closer to God than we already are. God is after our hearts. He is after our love and trust. He keeps all of His promises in His timing and in His way. He is not obligated to respond to our requirements for signs and proofs. We don't always know what He is doing, but we can know based on the Word that whatever it is, it's good! If we subject ourselves to an object or a person as methods to hear from the Lord, we may find ourselves guilty of idolatry. This will never give us access to God. We can't buy Him as Simon tried to do in Acts 8:18, and we can't conjure Him up to fit our expectations. He is always present and He waits for us to believe on Him. In our journey with Jesus, He gives us Himself—free for the asking. We don't need prayer cloths or holy water to coax His involvement in our lives. We shouldn't depend on a ticket to a concert or a special song to encounter God's presence. Signs will follow our faithfulness.

God's presence replaces our need for proof. We don't need to worry about God proving anything to us. He's already proven everything to us through Jesus' love and sacrifice on the cross. If you want to see a miracle, pull out your phone and take a selfie, cuz there she is! You are a miracle- sure and true. The transformation Christ has accomplished in you is sometimes the only miracle that truly matters in the grand scheme of our testimony and witness to the world! Christ is our proof that God loves us. The Holy Spirit is our proof that Christ is near! Scripture confirms itself, so all we need to do is believe. We don't need to prove the existence of someone who is already there. We don't need signs and wonders from someone we are in constant communication with. Does God still preform miracles? Absolutely. Would I still trust Him even if He never performed another miracle? Most definitely. Affirmations and confirmations have their places, but they can never take the place of spending time with God and developing discernment to hear directly from Him. He longs to speak to us, personally and often. There is a difference between knowing God and knowing about God. When we know God, we begin to recognize His voice. I pray that we become women who believe and just take Christ at His word, without the aid of signs.

Rich Girls

I used to watch a TV show about an heiress and her friend who would do common jobs you'd think they'd have had experience with as thirty-year-olds. But tasks like mopping the floor, plunging a toilet, or making their own bank deposits were too much for these poor, rich girls. It was humorous but also sort of sad. Despite the raises, the makeup, the new homes, and the bling; in truth, we are the poorest of people without Christ. We show off our assets and present our lives as prosperous to all our friends on social media, but underneath the name brands and the makeup, the tech gadgets, and the business cards, we can suffer spiritual calamity because of a lack of time spent with God. Our time spent with God makes us rich (see Luke 12:21). What we are missing is what will sustain us in the fire, hold us through the storm, cover our spiritual nakedness, and bring light to our confusion: God's truth. And His truth, though we sometimes try to avoid it, is the very thing that scripture likens to treasure (Matthew 12:35 and 13:52).

The very essence of truth and its origins are found in God, Himself. *"For the word of the Lord is right; and all his works are done in truth,"* the Word says in Psalm 33:4 (KJV). People who reject truth are rejecting God. It's a matter of both conviction and error. When we face truth, we see ourselves as God sees us. Then we humble ourselves in His sight and act with persistence to reflect Christ's nature. All of these things require selflessness—a state foreign to our flesh and distasteful to our selfish desires. In the name of tolerance, our culture has said "no" to the truths of God's Word and substituted in its place social approval. As Christians we have been called to a much higher life—a life not based on the gratification of the senses and the idolatry of self. Our lives are to be marked by the very essence of Christ's life, which only comes about from time spent with Him.

In Mark 10:17-27, Jesus confronts a young man who claimed to be on the quest for truth. The man approached Jesus and asked a simple question, *"What good thing must I do to receive eternal life?"* Jesus frankly presented the commandments to the young man who simply disregarded them. He felt justified that he had never offended any of the laws. Then Jesus tells the man to sell everything that he has and then follow Him. By this act he would find eternal life. But instead of being excited about following the Lord, scripture says the young man left saddened. He valued his earthly treasures above the truth. He didn't just walk away from *a* truth. He dismissed *The Truth*. He turned from Christ, Himself, because the call to turn from a life of self-gratification was uncomfortable.

Looking over this story, it has occurred to me that the quest to finding truth involves self-abandonment. Discovering truth requires not only the pursuit to know the Savior, but also a willingness to let go of all else. To find God, we must lose ourselves. To receive Heavenly riches, we must be willing to risk giving away our earthly ones. The rich young ruler held on too tightly to his own ideas of how to reach perfection. And these kept him from knowing the truth—who is Jesus, Himself (John 14:6). He did not recognize that his heart was filled with self-righteousness and pride. He lacked humility and faith. He depended on himself and not the Lord. Although he may not have stolen or murdered in his lifetime, had he even considered that he might have broken these commandments in his heart? Had he ever refused to forgive someone? That's spiritual murder. Had he ever coveted someone else's belongings? That's the same as thievery (see Proverbs 23:7 and Matthew 5:28).

The rich young ruler evaded the requirements for obtaining the truth. He was not willing to part with his riches because then he'd have nothing of which to cling. Riches provided a sense of security. And riches gave him an identity. They were his life—his dream. We look at his situation and pity him. We might say, "How sad for him. He could have encountered Heaven!" But the fact is, all of us have walked away from truth in one area or another and the call to obey it when we felt uncomfortable.

In each of us, there is a rich young ruler. Some of us are rich in our intellect and others in finances or friendships. Maybe we are rich because of social status or education. But when we come to terms with seeing the truth, which is Christ, the Son of God, do we avoid His call because of personal discomfort? Do we walk away because His requirements seem unrealistic or too difficult? Or, like the woman who lost her coin, do we search until we receive vast treasures from God? The time has come and will come again when we must face the truth about ourselves in light of God's Word. If we accept His truth despite difficulties and discomfort, the Bible says that a crown of glory awaits us (2 Timothy 4:8).

None of us will do it perfectly every time. We will miss opportunities to obey; and out of discomfort, we will hesitate from time to time. But through it all, the Lord is good and He'll keep calling us to live out His goodness, which is higher than ours. His truth is our treasure and when we obey, we reap a great reward from the Lord. Ladies, I don't know about you, but I want to be filthy rich in Christ! We are so needed in this generation. Our friends, sisters, and daughters need to see us living as vessels filled with treasures from the Word. They need to encounter women who prize God's truth in daily living. Our witness has the power to change lives! And we must desperately desire to see their lives changed for God's glory—as well as our own. I want to have the treasure of Heaven within my heart! I want to live a life where God's truth paves the way through any obstacle in store for me! What will your choice be? As we continue in our journey with Christ, remember that He is equipping you every step of the way. He has Kingdom agendas prepared for you and treasures that this world can never take away!

Growth

I remember clearly the first time I met my husband. It was the evening of a Wednesday night Bible study at the church we were both attending. I had been in Atlanta for a few weeks, filming a TV commercial, and my friends, Ashley and Kourtney, kept me up to date about the latest church gossip...I mean, "news." Apparently, there was a new guy at church for whom everyone was falling over themselves. According to Kourtney, he was the most good-looking guy who had come to church in a long time. He had "swagger," they told me. So naturally, you can understand my total shock when I came to church that Wednesday night to discover that Jarrett McCain, or "Saint" as he had been named in college, had long, messy dreadlocks and a stain on his shirt. I wasn't very impressed at first glance. Oh, but God had other plans!

At the time, my sights were set on ditching school and moving to New York. I had the opportunity to renew an old contract, but I was struggling with the decision whether to finish my program at UNC Greensboro or to dive into a New York state of mind. As I deliberated with my parents, I couldn't deny the impression to stay in North Carolina. A man was the very last thing in my sights, and if truth be told, there were already rumors going around that I was destined to marry someone else. I had no intentions of marrying anyone. I wanted to be a cover girl! I wanted New York and contracts and campaigns! I didn't have time for a boyfriend; I had my heart set on fame! In spite of it all, I felt the Lord urging me to stay put. It was a bitter decision, because it meant saying "no" to New York for the second time, and I knew there wouldn't be any more opportunities in the future. I was troubled because I wanted God to make those desires for New York a reality for me. I ached in my heart over being obedient, but I chose to stay put and trust the Lord with all that I had in me. As time went on, I signed a small local contract instead of the one I wanted so badly in Manhattan. Jarrett and I began developing a sweet friendship that would never have come forth had I left Greensboro, North Carolina. His frizzy hair didn't particularly win my vote at first sight, but the Lord corrected me in my vanity. His plans for me eclipsed superficial sights. Jarrett had a substance about him and a tenacity to his pursuit for Jesus. He was honest and kind, and I admired the way he volunteered his time and served others in church. He was genuine in the way he carried himself, and his appetite for God was very attractive!

Week by week, I saw small changes and transformations in him. I watched him clumsily lift his hands in worship, though he was clearly uncomfortable with doing so. He made me laugh when he would ask silly questions about Bible characters and he was so sincere in the way he treated my parents and in the friendship he began to develop with my brother. Our private conversations made my heart spin. "I don't know a lot about faith," Jarrett would say. "But I'm learning." His humility and hunger inspired me!

"What do you think about my man, Jarrett?" our friend Anthony Foster asked me one day. Other friends began asking similar questions to which I only replied with smiles. I knew that God was stirring my heart. I knew God had been stirring Jarrett's heart, as well. Before the end of the summer of 2010, Jarrett had cut his hair for a new job he'd just started and walked into church in a suit and tie. Lord have mercy! That's all I'm going to say!

Over the course of our three-year dating relationship, I witnessed this man change from baggy clothes to fitted suits. I quietly observed him grow from a naive curiosity into a confident faith in Christ. I watched God unveil Jarrett's heart and restore his life by the power of scripture and the love of Christ. His growth came through a willingness to seek Godly counsel and instruction from leaders he trusted, including my dad. He was open to correction and quick to admit when he was wrong. He made changes for God's glory, and He stood firmly on what he believed. As he drew nearer to the Lord, I was challenged in my own heart as well and, as a result, we focused more of our relationship on Jesus than on ourselves. We set curfews and boundaries to keep us obedient, and we asked friends to hold us accountable. On June 1, 2013, we rejoiced with all our loved ones over what God had done in our lives!

Four years of marriage and a beautiful daughter later, New York isn't even on my radar. Every day, Jarrett wears my purity ring on a chain around his neck. Our love illuminates our lives and I am filled with thankfulness. Each morning, I notice his quiet time with Jesus at the kitchen table, before heading off to work. He leads our family in prayer, supports all my eccentric projects, and is patient with me when I am difficult –which I often am. We have grown so much as a couple and in our spiritual relationship with Christ because we chose to obey. And we strive to continue to do so every day. Neither of us is perfect, but married life is radiant! As we continue to mature, I can look back and see what God has done! I have learned, and I keep learning, that the Lord's plans are so much better than mine. There was no love waiting for me in New York. I would have missed my husband if I hadn't followed the direction of the Holy Spirit. I would have missed my own growth and the chance to witness Jarrett's transformation, as well.

Although we are each on an individual journey with Jesus, we all should be in a place of continual development. We cannot claim maturity without evidence of growth. Christ desires to transform our lives through our obedience and transparency with Him. God's desire is to produce perpetual growth in us and this is accomplished twofold: on the one hand, He encourages us; and on the other, we undergo His correction. The two experiences are essential for healthy spiritual development. So often, however, we embrace encouragement but shun correction, because we are beings who are embarrassed to fail. We don't like correction because it reminds us that we are imperfect. So, we often hide difficult truths about ourselves to try and look the part. We don't want anyone to know that we are struggling or that we aren't as far along as they think we are. But Christ is not concerned when we are not living up to our own personal expectations of spiritual improvement. He isn't disappointed that we are not farther along than we thought we would be. He is more concerned that our hearts' desire be more of Him, so we can become more like Him.

What I truly admired in Jarrett was that he never hid his struggles. He never pretended to know things he didn't know. He didn't present himself as more than who he was. If he didn't know, he admitted it; if he wanted to know, he'd ask. Because Jarrett came from a broken home, a successful marriage was very important to him, so he insisted that we participate in marriage ministry at church, even before our engagement. Throughout our relationship, we were constantly attending pre-marital conferences and seminars. Many times we walked away from meetings knowing that we needed to realign our priorities or forgive one another for a past mistake. What we gained from those classes was God-sent correction and advice. It was up to us to incorporate and apply the wisdom to areas in our lives where we knew we needed to grow. This is a lesson for us all. Growth requires that we operate in honesty as the Lord reveals areas for change. Covering our struggles and failings doesn't conceal our weaknesses; it only perpetuates them. Christ invites us to be transparent with Him in all areas we deal with, so that His light will shine—exposing anything that is not of Him. The intimacy He seeks to establish with us then happens. We can share our hearts before the Lord because He is merciful and kind! He is very aware of what lies within us, and He beckons us to release it all to Him. God wants to meet us exactly where we are, but we must be honest with our own evaluation of ourselves in order to experience growth and maturity in our souls.

The Lord promises in Ezekiel 36:26, *"Moreover, I will give you a new heart and put a new spirit within you; and I will remove your heart of stone and give you a heart of flesh"* (NASB). In our journey with Jesus, we undergo spiritual heart transplants, continuously. His heart becomes our own as we grow more and more in our relationship with Him. In this way, we encounter victory, in Jesus' name, as we develop into all that He has purposed for us! It's critical to be transparent and depend on Him. Through faith and prayer, God's presence influences our circumstances. He teaches us to exemplify Him in ways we might never have before. It's His will to mature us and raise us up, but not for our glory—for His! He is the Eternal One. Whatever He creates will never end. If we want to be effective in our lives for Christ, it will take more than a "good-night" prayer and some nice deeds. Growth requires a change of heart and transformation through transparency as we are corrected and encouraged in Christ. Hebrews 12:7-8 declares, *"My dear child, don't shrug off God's discipline, but don't be crushed by it either. It's the child he loves that he disciplines; the child he embraces, he also corrects. God is educating you; that's why you must never drop out. He's treating you as dear children. This trouble you're in isn't punishment; it's training, the normal experience of children"* (MSG).

Many of us make the mistake of associating discipline with punishment. We perceive it as a negative consequence, rather than a loving gift from our Heavenly Father. In Christ, we aren't corrected for punishment. God's discipline positions us for growth in order to build our character. As we maneuver our lives in Christ, God extracts impurities from our hearts by revealing to us what He longs to change. Although sometimes difficult to accept and uncomfortable to admit, let's not fool ourselves into the naïve belief that the discomfort from discipline isn't part of God's plan for our good. Sometimes, my loves, it is. Sometimes, our tears are necessary for our development. But He loves us through it and keeps a record of each and every precious tear we cry (Psalm 56:8).

Immaturity will always urge us to avoid the changes Christ desires. We think by avoidance we won't have to face the trials or the disciplinary measures of God. But women who desire more of the Lord accept the challenges of change. There are lessons that we must learn to be the women we've been called to be! Christ's invitation of transformation may sometimes feel challenging, and the trials we find ourselves in can seem overwhelming, but scripture tells us it is necessary for our growth. In every season of life, there will come a time for toil, but it's the toil that produces prosperous lives! Correction isn't always easy. It's a tedious process of change and transformation. But this loving discipline will develop our character such that we can stand in the responsibilities that go with our destinies! If we desire to grow and prosper, then we must have hearts that embrace the discipline of the Lord.

Sharing Your Story

In March 2015, the women of Pearls of Hope Outreach had the beautiful opportunity to travel to Roatan, Honduras, for a mission trip. My father led our group during the Zika Virus scare and although there were concerns about safety, we enjoyed a very rewarding and challenging experience. For many of us, it was our first time out of the country. Our preparation consisted of fundraising, fasting, and weekly training sessions. In each session, we undertook the process of learning how to share our testimonies. If you are familiar with church life, a testimony is a personal story you share about what God has done for you. In our mission training, we practiced sharing our entire story of transformation in Christ: who we were before Christ, how we met Christ, and who we are becoming after our encounter with Christ.

It seemed easy at first. Most of us had known each other before Pearls of Hope. We were among close friends, but being totally transparent with ourselves, as well as with our peers, was challenging. It was intimidating, to be honest. For me, especially, I was worried over sharing some truths that I knew my father had no awareness of. There were thirteen of us on the team. Though the training was intense, the broken chains, freedom in Christ, and stories of salvation pulled us together into a deeper spiritual unity. We laid hands on each other, cried over victories, extended forgiveness where necessary and moved into realms of unknown territory with confidence. The success of this particular trip wasn't based on speeches given in a far off country or money raised to bless children in need. It came from simply allowing

God full control to release His Spirit as we shared our experiences of His transforming power!

Transparency with God produces transparency with others, and this openness builds a platform for incredible witnessing opportunities. The Lord is doing a mighty work in us all and we should give Him credit for the good things He has done. Our testimonies affirm to the world the saving power of Christ! His light shines brightest in our midnight moments, and when day finally begins to break, we see how far we've come. Our salvation should excite us into sharing encouragement with others! Yet, so often, we are too timid to declare the goodness of the Lord, apart from clichés or shallow praises. Yes, thank God for your car and the clothes on your back, but what about His delivering power over your addiction, or how He transformed your mind from the destruction of manipulation or greed? These are the stories that make lasting impacts on hearts who need to know there is hope in Christ for them! Concealing our development won't give God glory. Churchy platitudes of, "I might stumble, but I'll never fall," couldn't be further from the truth. Each day, we do fall in some way, because we are imperfect people. We are all in the same boat, apart from Christ, and those of us who are in Christ should have a burden in our hearts to reach out in love to those who need Him. Society doesn't want our pity or our judgments; they need to hear our stories. They need to know we were once lost and falling apart. They need to know that we struggle in sin, but Jesus came to free us from our failures. They need to hear the truth of what God has done for us, and what He can do for them. We can sabotage our own growth and relationships by pretending to be something or someone we're not. God doesn't get the glory out of our exaggerations. There are people who need to hear your *true* story! There are communities that will find encouragement from the lessons you've learned and the maturity you've found in your journey with Jesus.

Each of our stories is unique and significant. My journey in Christ may differ from yours, in many ways, but the central theme for us all is Jesus. No matter who we were before we met the Lord, we can all walk in the same victory granted to us from the same cross. That is why we must constantly depend upon the Savior who saves! Every moment of every day we are saved, we are being saved, and we have the promise that when Christ returns, we will be abundantly saved! Amen! When we share our stories, we must do so with honest humility. Fake humility is still fake. Be truthful about what God has done in your life; and when you find yourself with an opportunity to share, do so in love (see Ephesians 4:15). This is our mission! How can we expect success in future ministry if we aren't ministering successfully to people in our current lives? Never be ashamed of the lessons God is guiding you through. The truth is powerful. It will free us to fulfill our calling and release others into theirs. Allow the Lord to use your experiences to develop others. Your story could bring life to those who feel unworthy. Your story could change a person's understanding of what God can do for them. All of us who now walk with Christ, did so as a result of someone else's testimony. Someone was courageous enough to tell us that God loves us and can change us. Each of our relationships with Jesus began by observing the life of another believer. And if we're honest, in many cases, it was a testimony of overcoming imperfection that attracted us to God.

Ladies, listen, the world isn't looking for more pretty little liars. They are looking for women of valor—women who accept the call to walk in honesty and love others courageously, like Christ. God calls women who aren't afraid to kick their heels off, roll up their sleeves, and help someone out of the same pit into which they once fell. Fancy words and cute clothes won't change hearts. Our imperfections can produce the platform God desires to show off His transforming power within us. His perfection is a process that goes on into eternity; though we fall, we are not forsaken. Sharing our stories might seem scary to those of us who are just beginning to open up about our faith, but our confidence isn't in ourselves. We share knowing that God has chosen us to shine His light so that others will be drawn to Himself. Yes, there is always risk in revealing ourselves, but there is greater danger in pretense. Many hearts have been badly damaged because those around them chose to parade a "perfect image" instead of sharing their stories with truth.

We've each come a long way, but we're not done yet. We are on a journey that involves rising and falling from time to time. Some of us have been through hell. Some of us are still going through the fire, and some of us know of others also walking through seasons of difficulty. There may be tough days ahead, but there are also tremendous victories to be won and shared!

As we stand in faith and declare the goodness of God, Heaven will begin to open up! Revival can take place, even if only in the heart of one person. Scripture tells us that all of Heaven rejoices, even over one soul who comes to Christ (Luke 15:7). Your story could be the encouragement someone needs to take steps towards the cross! Your scars are proof of God's healing, and your testimony could bring the ointment of the Spirit for the lost and hurting in this world. As we sojourn on, we will meet many hearts and souls along the way. Some will enter our lives to speak encouragement over us; some will need our love for their encouragement and growth in Christ. We will always be on the receiving and giving end when it comes to being built up in the Lord. It's our growth that inspires others. Our stories and testimonies of how God has triumphed in our lives *will* make a difference for His kingdom! As we grow and develop in our journey with Jesus, we gain some pretty awesome stories to tell—stories of God's beautiful redemption, transformation, and love! Ask God to build your confidence as you courageously share your story of salvation and His loving kindness and goodness in your life.

Completely Loved

I think we all have areas when we question our own worth and value. It's always that one situation where we can't seem to find relief—that one circumstance where our best efforts don't seem to be good enough. Over the last year, I have suffered from cruel words and hostile lies that were aimed to belittle me and tear me down. As a result, I allowed offense and the root of bitterness to grow inside my heart and I let my pain and disappointment produce resentment, when I should have just surrendered it. I've often prayed for Christ to weed out these roots, because they keep growing back.

On one particular night, I came to God with my head held low, dropping tears like atom bombs onto the floor. The rage I wrestled with was crippling me and I shook with shame as I prayed to my Heavenly Father. I needed to know that I was still loved, in spite of the anger that had wedged within my heart. I needed to know that my bitterness and my brokenness didn't make me ugly in His sight. I sought assurance that He still looked at me with love, despite the dreadful feelings and resentment I was struggling with.

So often, we fear the disgrace of imperfection, but "Loved" is the new perfect! Christ declares that we are truly cherished and loved and treasured! The beauty of salvation through God's grace is that it is completely and utterly based on that fact that Jesus adores us and it's for this reason that He endured the cross. He knows we will fall in the mud and thicket of sin in this world. It will have its effect on us, in one way or another: hatred, deception, addiction, greed... they all are results of living in this fallen world. Jesus is not asking you to perfect yourself or to hide your sin from Him. Rather, He desires to be invited in, so that He can begin the process of perfecting your heart with each prayer you pray, each experience you live through and every scripture you obey. He longs to exchange His beauty for your ashes (Isaiah 61:3).

Never let your lack of goodness hinder you from the God who loves you. We don't have to hide the scars that still aren't healed. God sees all, and He loves us, regardless. Each of us have been called with a purpose according to God's goodness and love, and nothing, even our lack, can hinder Him. Nothing can separate us from His love. Romans 8:38-39 tells us, "*For I am convinced that neither death nor life, neither angels nor principalities, neither the present nor the future, nor any powers, neither height nor depth, or anything else in all creation, will be able to separate us from the love of God that is in Christ Jesus our Lord*" (NIV).

For the better part of my twenties, I searched to discover what was worth loving in me. I searched frantically for the parts of me that were completely and totally acceptable. What in me was beautiful to others? What in me was beautiful to myself? While seeking to answer these questions, I lost pieces of myself by leaving God out. I got sucked into the miserable abyss of altering myself in order to gain a sense of worth from others. If I'm honest, I still struggle with this. I still struggle with being completely me in the midst of those who don't quite get me. Maybe you do, too. But Jesus never called us to abandon the woman

He created us to be. He loves us completely as we are in every moment of our existence. We can know that salvation in Christ doesn't erase who we are. Rather, by living for Christ, His Spirit brings forth our true selves. He shapes us into being who He purposed us to be from the very beginning. Voices will tell us that we will never be "good" enough, that we aren't relatable, or that we don't fit in. But it's through God's eyes that we see our worth and value. We have to stop basing our opinions about ourselves on the opinions of others.

People will speak many labels over us and call us by many names. But as we face ourselves in the light of Christ, the only true title over us is "Loved." We are called "Loved" by God, Himself! We are cherished and celebrated! Scripture tells us that God delights and dances and sings over us! Zephaniah exults in 3:17, *"For the LORD your God is with you. He is a mighty savior. He will take delight in you with gladness. With His love, He will calm all your fears. He will rejoice over you with joyful songs"* (NLT).

We are His joy and the object of His devotion. God loves us greater in one moment than anyone could ever love us in a lifetime! Never forget that. It's a true mystery that Christ passionately and completely loves us—you and me. It's not by our goodness, because we have none; not really. We are truly imperfect, through and through, yet, God loves everything about us: past, present, and future. He does not love our present selves more than He loves our past selves. He doesn't love our past selves any more or any less than our future selves. We are completely and totally loved as we are, for who we are, and where we are. As we receive this unconditional love of God, it transforms our existence from a state of simply being into a state of being perfected in the beauty and grace of Christ. We are royalty because our Eternal Father is the King of the universe!

We are beautiful because Christ radiates gloriously from within us. Outside of Jesus, we live half versions of our true identities, but in Him, we are incandescent!

It's a wondrous thing to know that the most beautiful person who has ever existed notices us, wants us, and waits for us to receive Him completely just as He receives us. There is no place we can go or hide where Jesus Christ can't find us. There is no depth to which we can fall where His love cannot catch us. But receiving Christ does require our accepting His invitation.

Understanding our true worth involves humbling our hearts and embracing the reality that we are neither above nor below anyone. We can become greater than we are or we can operate beneath the potential that God has placed within us, but this reflects our decisions—not our worth. We are always in a perpetual state of being loved. Say to yourself, "I am loved by God." Say it again, out loud, and believe it this time. You are loved. You are not loved for your sense of humor, your dress size, or for your accomplishments. You are simply loved because God created you in His image and He has placed His Spirit in you. And all that God has created, He declares as good (see Genesis 3:1).

Jesus did not die to make you the better version of the self that you think you ought to be. God's wisdom and His plans for us far exceed the best of anything we could intend. In our moments of frustration and mood swings, we are still loved. When we ache with self-pity and disappointment over people who misunderstand us, Jesus is not annoyed. He is moved with compassion. Regardless of where we've been, who we've hurt, or who has hurt us, we can count on God's love. Even if others don't see that we wear robes of righteousness, it really makes no difference (Isaiah 61:10 NIV). Journeying on with Jesus isn't about making ourselves better people. It's about God's divine desire to walk in relationship with us through Jesus and the victorious power of the Holy Spirit. He invites us to be a part of His amazing love, regardless of the person we are or used to be. That doesn't change who we are to Him. Our Savior is for us, and His love makes us glorious! God has stamped His approval on us. He calls us daughters and beckons us on into a wonderful journey where we are completely loved with every step we take in Him.

Questions for Discussion

1. Please read 1John 4:19, and record it in the space below.

   What does this Scripture mean to you? How can you apply it in your daily life as you journey deeper into a love relationship with Jesus?

2. Have you ever shared your testimony with others? Were you intimidated to do so? Would you be willing to share your personal testimony on the spot if someone asked you to?

   Below, write out your story of God's grace and ask the Lord to guide you to opportunities to share your testimony for the encouragement of others.

   Who were you before you received Christ? What did you do? How did you live?

   How did you encounter Christ? Did you say a prayer in church? Did a family or loved one introduce you to Jesus? Did you learn about salvation from TV or the radio?

   How has your life changed since you've accepted Jesus? How has your attitude or mindset changed? What about your actions and lifestyle? What about you is different now as a result of living for Christ?

3. "God loves you greater in one moment than anyone could ever love you in a lifetime!" What impact does this statement make on you? Is this a truth that you can easily accept, or are you still finding it difficult to believe that you are completely loved by God? Reflect on ways that you have experienced God's love or seen God show His love in the lives of others.

CHAPTER 10

Encouragement from Yours Truly

When I finally got the nerve to ask my husband to read this book, he asked me what my overall goal was for publication. My immediate response was that I wanted to encourage my friends. I told him, "I'll probably never meet the people who'll read this book, but at least they'll get to meet me and know that someone in North Carolina loves them!" It sounds silly, but I honestly just have a heart for people. I love people, and I love being a friend. I hope you got a sense of my friendship throughout these pages. I hope that I have shown you God's love and encouraged you to love Him authentically, despite our culture, which tells us that we can't. I'd love to pray over you now!

Dear Lord,

In Jesus' name, I bless my sister, and I ask, Father, that You will pour out all of Your promises on her. She may be in a season of waiting or in a low valley right now. Maybe she is rejoicing or still trying to figure out her decision for You. Regardless of where she is, Lord, please let her know that You are there. Please pour out Your consuming fire over all of her efforts, her dreams, and doubts. Show her who You are and who You want to be in her life.

Lord, I lift up each sweet heart that is reading this book, and I pray that your Spirit will comfort, encourage and position everyone for their God-appointed destiny. I cast down each and every stronghold that the enemy desires to use to distract. His fiery arrows have no power over my sisters! His lies and deceptions no longer have an invitation into their minds, hearts, or lives. I pray for reconciliation in families, Lord. I ask for the gift of marriage for my sisters. I pray for healing over broken hearts and wounded souls. I pray over cancer, infertility, debt, fear, and doubt. I pray over every regret and every tear. I pray for continued victory, revelation and realization of vision and of your calling over my sisters! I ask, in Jesus name, that ministries be birthed and produced, as a result of your presence in their lives. I ask you Lord to bless their families and prosper their futures. I lift all these up to You, Lord, because each woman is so dearly loved by You.

Jesus, radiate within them. Produce the treasure of Heaven in their hearts—the treasure of simply falling madly in love with You! Give them confidence for their daily lives. Give them grace for their journeys and the hope of eternity in their hearts. Raise up your daughters to succeed with greatness and with grace at whatever their fingers touch. Lavish them with your love, Father.

I thank You for their hearts. I thank You for bestowing Your goodness upon them, and I pray that they take up the call to love like you and live for you, one day at a time.

In Jesus' name,

Amen

My heart was burning to pray over you! You are never alone. Many prayers circulate in Heaven on your behalf. You have had heavenly encounters throughout your entire life, whether you're aware of these encounters or not. Christ has been at work in you. He desires to take you higher; He wants to move you from glory to glory! His love for you compels Him to lead you into ever greater things, so don't be intimidated by those steps of obedience He asks you to take. The world is holding its breath for a miracle; they are waiting to see God's love! You have been called to show it to them. You are equipped and prepared in Christ. So embrace your calling, and stand firm in the fact that you have a purpose in Christ! Live beyond your unmet expectations. Put more faith in God's promises than in people's requirements. Once you do, I promise you will begin to see things in a different light.

The Call of Salvation

A few weeks ago, I sat across from a sweet girl who wanted to know what salvation is all about. It's surprising that many self-proclaimed "church girls" or "good girls" aren't sure about their eternal salvation. They question if their salvation is secured. But we can know for sure, in Jesus' name! Our salvation is only affirmed at the foot of the cross. Jesus came to die for our sins because our sins were killing us, literally and figuratively. So God, in His abundant love, desperately desired to win us back. So He came down to earth as a person and died for us so that we could have eternal life (see 1 Thessalonians 5:10).

Nothing outside of a relationship with Jesus will remove our unrighteousness. Sitting on a pew on Sunday is not going to save us from our sins. Water can clean our bodies, but it can't clean our spirits. Reading books is great for encouragement, but books can't replace our need for Christ. We can't do enough good things or donate enough money to escape the death due us because of our sin. We are not enough on our own.

Once we realize our state, salvation in Christ can have full effect. We simply acknowledge that we need Jesus and receive Him into our lives. You don't have to get things right first. Honestly, you never will. All you need is an open heart, and Christ will do the rest. If any of you are willing to invite Jesus Christ to become your Savior, I'd love to pray with you! I'd love for you to invite Jesus into your heart, and begin your journey with Him today. It's a beautiful life, though not a perfect one. However, Christ is perfect, and He will transform you every step of the way!

Romans 10:9 tells us that if we confess with our mouths and believe in our hearts that Jesus is Lord and that God raised Him from the dead to save our sins, then we will have salvation. I invite those of you who are willing to receive Jesus Christ as Lord, to say this prayer, out loud, as a confession with your mouth. Let's go to God together. Pretend that I am holding your hand!

Dear Jesus,

I know that you are the Son of God, and I believe that You died on the cross for my sins because You love me. I want Your perfect love to dwell in my heart forever, so I ask You to come and save me. I want to be born again and receive the new nature of Christ. I can't be good on my own. I've tried, but I am an imperfect person and I sin every day. I want to live a life that is pleasing to You, and I want to be close to You and have a relationship with You. Thank You for loving me, even in my sin. I know that You have made me a new creation and that my past will never hold me back from the future that You have for me. Thank You for the Holy Spirit given to guide me. Teach me how to love as You do. Thank You for Your healing, complete forgiveness, and grace. Please connect me with others who will support me and encourage me to live every day for You!

In Jesus' name, I pray.

Amen.

Sign and date below:

____

____

Yay! I'm so excited for you! Welcome to the family of God! Those of you who decide to receive Jesus, please email me and tell me all about it! I'd love to hear from you! For some of you, this might be your first time praying for salvation. For others, maybe it's your third or fifth time. No matter. Whenever we call upon God with sincere hearts, He hears and answers us! It's His joy to give the gift of salvation and lavish His love and promises on those who bear the name of Christ! I suggest that you get plugged into a local church. Get involved. Contact a pastor, or a trusted family member or friend whom you know is living for Jesus. The Christian journey is not an independent one; you'll need support and help along the way. Christ will lead you to connections with those who will encourage you. Don't be afraid to ask for help. Tell someone about your news of salvation in Christ! Congratulations, honey! You've made the best decision you could ever make!

Prayers for Purity

Even after salvation and the beginning of our new lives in Jesus, our culture will not stop at trying to convince us that we are not new creations in Christ. This is a lie. You are a new creation! The Bible says so in 2 Corinthians 5:17, *"Therefore, if anyone is in Christ, he is a new creation. The old has passed away; behold, the new has come"* (ESV). People might occasionally remind you of who you used to be, but you are no longer that person, once your heart belongs to Christ. Now, you embody His perfection and His purity in your life. I want to encourage you that it is possible to be pure! I am living proof that virginity is possible until marriage, but purity is possible for a lifetime!

So many of you lived unaware of God's good plans of marriage and obeyed what the songs on the radio told you to do. You admired worldly women on TV and caved into peer pressure from your boyfriends and peers. You soaked up magazines that celebrated "free sex" and taught you the top ten ways to make your sex life sizzle. But they never explained to you the destruction that sex outside of marriage would cause on your heart once it was over. The enemy never prepares you for the consequences. Your hearts aren't shatterproof, and the pain felt from giving the sacred away leaves lasting marks. Don't be ashamed. You did what you were taught to do. You followed what the world teaches. It's not your fault. But now you are of a different world—the Kingdom of God. You are learning that His ways satisfy long term and bring protection and spiritual pleasure. His ways aren't for the passing moment because He is an eternal God. His blessings are everlasting when we obey Him.

I also realize that there are some of you out there who were robbed of your choice to save your sacredness. I recognize that selfish lust and greed has taken a toll on so many innocent hearts. But you are not disqualified from purity, either. This is God's gift of restoration: that all hearts can be made clean and pure! What was done to you by sinful choices wasn't your fault. You are no less beautiful in God's eyes than the virgin bride. He loves you and He longs to heal you and restore you, despite the pain you've endured. Hold your head up high! You are royalty!

Listen, if you've never heard it before, you're going to hear it now from me: Your body is sacred. Your love and your life are sacred. You are not someone's fantasy. You don't have to go through the motions of giving yourself away in hopes of securing stability or affection. The world says you can't go back, but in Christ you can! There is always a road that leads back to Him—a road of promise for pleasures beyond a Friday night. Remember, we aren't living for "now". Wisdom sees the future and counts the cost, ahead of time. Just because you've made unwise choices in the past, doesn't mean you are obligated to continue to make them. Your future is at stake, so is your health, your peace of mind and your relationship with Christ and with others.

According to Gary Thomas, author of *The Sacred Marriage* and *The Sacred Search*, sexual involvement before marriage is a strong indicator that each individual is actually operating in selfishness and will not have the stamina of *selflessness* required to endure a loving and lasting marriage. He states, "*If your dating relationship is sustained by sin, what will sustain your marriage?*" It's something to definitely ponder, because, we all want lasting love, but, "*If your* *[current relationship] isn't motivated by God, there's not enough about you to keep [them] interested...this might shock you, but your best chance at sexual satisfaction in marriage is...virtue."**

I can honestly tell you that this has been the case in my marriage. Marital sex is not boring; it's a blessing (hallelujah)! We've been conditioned to believe that sex fades in marriage, but if done God's way, it's the exact opposite case (see 1 Corinthians 7:3-4). In my personal experiences, it was the times where I compromised that ultimately destroyed the relationship I thought I was saving. But there is freedom and lasting joy in purity and virtue! I'm urging you to wait on the man whom God says is best for you, who will selflessly love you and honor you, because you are worth that wait! Yes, waiting can be draining. It will sometimes feel as if you are missing out, but deep down you know this isn't true. You aren't missing out on anything when you walk in purity before God. In actuality, you are dodging bullets—bullets aimed to bring worry, fear and regret. Such chaos was never in God's original plan for you. We see our friends constantly in and out of relationships. Some go three months with this person and seven months with that person, only to give themselves away time and again with no results to show for it. Some of you know the fear of STD's or STI's. You've worried about unplanned pregnancy or being cheated on and taken for granted. That is not God's abundant life for you. God created you to be cherished, not used. You were created for freedom, not fear. You are more than just a girlfriend. You are a Kingdom woman and should be treated accordingly, not just from others, but also from yourself.

God knew what He was doing when He set the parameters of marriage around sex. He was thinking about your total well-being—mind, body, heart, and soul. Our emotions are delicate, and abstinence

---

* Gary Thomas, *The Sacred Search* (Colorado Springs: David Cook, 2013), 48.

protects them. Celibacy unto the Lord is a good thing. No condom can protect your heart, your mind, or your spirit; only our obedience and love for Christ can shield us. God created sex to be enjoyed, and it is enjoyable! But God is a God of order, and His restrictions are for our health and safety as well as our pleasure. In marriage, there is a freedom of intimacy and vulnerability without any inhibitions or limitations. God has planned for your sex life to take place in the covenant of marriage with a man who will love you as radically and unconditionally as Christ does.

My biggest mistake before I was married was putting more emphasis on virginity than on purity. Virginity is physical, but purity is spiritual. I hope that gives some of you hope and erases any disgrace that you may be carrying. Don't fall prey to the lie that you can't be pure. Yes, you most certainly can! Through salvation, God's holiness becomes your holiness, and you are clean because of Christ! You are free from your past sins, past partners, past shame, and regrets! I've had so many conversations with girls who feel defeated. They think they could never wait until marriage because they've done too much or gone too far. They are broken from their choices of giving themselves away for temporary gratification. But see, we are all broken—every single one of us. I might have been a virgin, but I was still broken. We each have suffered in our lives because of sin and the sin of sexual impurity is one that has affected us all, to some degree. We aren't perfect. We've had failed relationships, drug problems, anger issues, abusive pasts, pornography, anorexia, bulimia, hate, low self-esteem, jealousy.... it goes on and on. Yet our identities aren't synonymous with our brokenness. We are who God says we are, and He says we are beloved! There is no shame or regret when we live our lives God's way. But the choice and responsibility is up to us.

If you'd like to make a commitment to Christ concerning your purity by waiting until marriage, I'd love to pray with you! It doesn't matter if you've had twenty partners or none at all. It's never too late or too early to walk in purity. If you're already married, you can still take a stance on purity as well! Marriage is a holy institution; it's a covenant established to mirror God's unfailing love and salvation. As wives, we are called to love our husbands with respect and nobility, as a reflection of how we are to love God (Ephesians 5:22). Our culture often attacks this mission and, if we are not intentional about operating in purity within our marriages, we could easily find ourselves mistreating the men we've so earnestly prayed for.

Whether single or married, purity is necessary for us all. The Scripture that I often recited to myself during my waiting season was Psalms 119:9, *"How can a young person stay on the path of purity? By living according to your word"* (NIV).

Dear Lord,

I know that Your ways are only for my good and that You alone know the future. You have purposed great things for me. The world pressures me into giving my love away at my convenience or for the convenience of others, but Lord, I believe Your Word that my body is Your temple and that my heart is sacred to You. I want to honor You in the way I handle my body and in the way I give my love. I know that marriage is Your institution designed out of Your love for me. You are committed to me. You sacrificed for me—Your love for me isn't selfish or temporary. Lord, that is the love that I want reflected in my life. Teach me to wait for the time when You will lead me to the person who will love me as You do. Lord, I lift up my future husband, in Jesus name! I ask Lord that You will fill him with Your spirit and love. I pray over his ambitions and his family. I pray over his education, his finances, his friendships, and his relationship with You! Cause him to pursue You like never before. I pray for my heart as well, that I will obey as I wait for your perfect plan to unfold. Give me Your love and strength to do what is right in Your sight and grace me to honor You in my love life.

In Jesus name,

Amen.

Sign and date below:

____

____

True Promises

Throughout this book, we've discussed the blessings in store when we walk in obedience to God. In His word, He assures us of this, so as we move forward in our salvation, we can do so in confidence that we have much to receive from The Lord! *"And because of His glory and excellence, He has given us great and precious promises. These are the promises that enable you to share His divine nature and escape the world's corruption"* (2 Peter 1:4 NIV).

God promises to bless us if we follow His instructions. Although every promise has a premise, the condition attached ushers in permanent blessings in our relationship with Jesus and our influence in our world. Never let anyone ever tell you that you are doing "too much" for Christ. I rebuke anyone in Jesus' name who would ever dare tell you that it doesn't take "all that" to be a Christian. It most certainly does take all that. It takes all our love, all our faith, and all our prayers to impact the world for the cause of Jesus! The difference is in the heart.

When we love our Lord, giving our all is our joy and delight. But if we choose to hold back out of convenience or intimidation, we are really holding back from God and a total experience of His promises for us. A hindered heart reflects a lack of total trust. But our God is trustworthy! His promises are sure.

> *"God is ever true to His promises, and it was by Him that you were, one and all, called into fellowship with his Son Jesus Christ, our Lord"* (1 Corinthians 1:9 WNT).

To each of us, God has purposed and destined incomparable things. We each have our own calling and our own destiny. God asks for our all and our best because He has given His best to us through the blessing and promise of Jesus! Daily, we are being transformed by the Spirit of love, life, and truth! Our desire is that no one lives in darkness any longer than they need to. This requires us to stay consistently on our knees in prayer and to seek God's face in bringing us opportunities to pour out His love on others. As a result, His promises can go forth from our hearts in very visible ways.

> *"Lord, you have stored up great blessings for those who honor you. You do much for those who come to you for protection, blessing them before the watching world."* Psalm 31:19 (NLT)

God's goodness, through us, makes the difference. We are wonderfully complicated, special, and cherished. On our worst days, God has promised that we are dearly loved. We can exhale as our "goodness" does not affect our salvation. It's in Christ alone that we have victory over temptations and struggles. We can pray confidently for a greater capacity to love and for greater faith—these things God longs to bestow on us. As we seek the Lord for His direction, our hearts and actions begin to change. They come into accord with His will for us and His plans for those around us. The gift of salvation is the ultimate promise, and we have been blessed to be the recipients!

Perfectly Imperfect

By now, I hope you know that we are all in this together. None of us are perfect. None of us will ever be, but God's perfection is more than enough for any area, situation, or circumstance in our lives. My desire for each of us is expressed by what Paul wrote in Ephesians 3:16-18:

> *"I pray that out of his glorious riches he may strengthen you with power through his Spirit in your inner being, so that Christ may dwell in your hearts through faith. And I pray that you, being rooted and established in love, may have power, together with all the LORD's holy people, to grasp how wide and long and high and deep is the love of Christ"* (NIV).

The mystery in Jesus is that someone so perfect would love someone so imperfect. We have nothing to offer to Christ, yet we are all He desires. I will never quite grasp the totality of God's love, but I sure am thankful! As we part ways, I want to be sure and encourage you to stay strong in the Lord and rest in the assurance that you need do nothing except love Jesus and be loved by Him. May you begin to rely on God's goodness, and not your own, as you journey with Jesus. His perfection is the only lasting thing, and His love will fill up all of our emptiness and tattered places. Nothing compares with the beauty that lies ahead for each of us once we trust our hearts to our trustworthy God and allow His love to perfect our lives from the inside out. His goodness is all we need and His perfection will progress in our hearts in ways unimaginable, if we but trust and obey Him. This is what will separate us from the "good girls"! His presence, through our obedience, will result in a radical life of love and purpose. You are cherished, in spite of your mistakes, in spite of your frustrations and in spite of any hindrances you may face. Rest assured that Christ's love is enough and in Him is where true beauty lies. It's His perfect love in our imperfect hearts that will lead us to living a life that goes beyond being good. He eagerly invites you on this life-changing journey. Are you ready?

Questions for Discussion

1. We know that salvation is not a state of mind. We actually must confess our sins and receive God's gift of salvation by inviting Jesus into our lives (Romans 10:9). Reflect on the moment you received Jesus into your life. Was it at church or in your home? Who led you to Christ? How has your life changed since your new birth? Or if you are still considering God's offer of salvation through His Son, Jesus, are there some people who are encouraging you? What does their example of life in Christ look like?

2. Please record 1 Corinthians 5:17 below. What is this Scripture saying? How does it apply to you and your relationship with Jesus?

3. The literal translation of the word "Gospel" means "good news!" It is good news that God's love isn't dependent on our being perfect "good girls." His love is greater than our incapacity for perfection. None of us are perfect, and none of us will ever be until Christ's work is finished. But we are perfectly loved by God, and His love goes beyond being good.

   Below, please write out your own prayer to the Lord. Thank Him for His love for you. Lift up various areas in your life where you need His love to cover you. Know that you are not alone.

ALL MY LOVE TO YOU

Acknowledgements

Writing this book has been such a sweet experience for me. I publicly thank those below who have helped in my development as a person as well as a writer. My love for you cannot be contained.

To Jarrett, my loving husband: Thank you for your relentless and ferocious love for me. Thank you for your sincerity and consistency in loving me like Christ even when I'm difficult. I see Jesus in your eyes every day, and our marriage has been one of God's sweetest gifts to me. Every day you submerge me in grace, and with you, I know I belong. I appreciate you, and I respect you beyond any words I could write or say. Thank you for believing that I am the most beautiful woman in the world and for investing in my dreams and supporting my calling. I am honored to raise Kailyn beside you. I'm ecstatic about building our legacy together. We are Forever Blessed. I love you!

To Benjamin, my brother and my heart: Thank you for always being the strong one. Thank you for reminding me to keep the main thing the main thing. You've kept my secrets and corrected me as needed. You've celebrated each phase of life with me, and you've grown into such a beautiful man. I'm so very proud to call you brother. In Christ, we are bound with a bond beyond our bloodline. You *are* God's best and have been appointed for amazing things! I am always on your side; thanks for always being on mine. You have truly been one of the greatest examples of how the love of Christ can transform a life. You are the youngest, but I greatly look up to you and admire your maturity in Christ.

To Reggie and Fran, my sweet parents: Thank you for your legacy of love and excellence. Thank you for your example of discipline and wisdom. Thank you for being my saints in the flesh and for raising me with love and responsibility while exemplifying the real Jesus every day of my life. Mommy, thank you for raising me to be a lady and not just a female. Thank you for Bible story examples and for setting high standards for me. Thank you for always telling me that I can come to you about anything or anyone. Thank you so much for that open door. Daddy, thank you for covering me in prayer when I was lost and confused in the world. And thank you for receiving me back to restoration after Christ came and found me. Thank you for our 2:00 a.m. talks and for being the greatest example in my life of my Heavenly Father. Thank you for being so involved in my academics as well as in my spiritual growth and development. I love you both immensely, and I hope I have made you proud.

To Jazzie, my favorite cousin: We aren't little girls anymore are we? From parties to prayer life, you've seen the transformation in me and loved me all along. Thank you for your faith. Thank you for offering accountability with honesty and for always finding something to laugh about! Your authentic hunger for Jesus has been a force to push me in my life. I thank the Lord for you and Montel! I love you both, and I am blessed that we are family. Not everyone knows the closeness of family the way we do. I am so glad that Jesus chose to allow us to share our lives together. I'm always praying for you, and I'm itching to see you again, soon!

To Andrea, the "New" Mrs. Coleman: Oh my darling, I love our sisterhood! I couldn't have picked a sweeter or kinder woman for my brother. Our family loves you so much and you have been an exciting addition! I'm thankful that I never had to earn your affection or prove myself to you. You've accepted me with kindness from the start and extended your friendship free of charge! Thank you for your beam of Jesus light that you shine so brightly! Thank you for your encouragement and your genuine love! Thank you for being so excited about this book! Thank you for all your words of encouragement and our weekly phone calls! You have been a balm to my heart, and I am so proud to be your sister-in-love! Cheers to the future and lots of babies!

To Ashley, my "Ride or Die": As friends come, you are a real one! Thank you for believing in my vision. Thank you for your daily check-ins, for being my number one go-to person in Pearls of Hope and for always being the one who tells me I'm doing a great job. I appreciate you more than ink could ever reveal. Thank you for enduring my crazy ideas and never questioning my ability. Thank you for always insisting that I let you help me. Thank you for always being that one person with whom I can laugh out loud even in inappropriate places! Thank you for driving up a mountain for me, for putting your neck on the line with me, for spending your hair appointment money on our projects, and for answering my 5:00 a.m. text messages about Pearls. Thank you for playing hooky from work with me and for letting me cry in times of need. I so cherish our chocolate dessert dates, and I so dearly love you!

To Pearls of Hope—my "PEARSLS" (lol): I love you all emphatically! Whether you came for a short time or have stuck it out for the long haul, every past and present member has been dear to my heart. Everything done for you has been done through Christ! I hope you know my love is real. You all awakened in me what I never knew existed. You've added so much drive and accomplishment to my life. I love "us" so much! Thank you for entrusting me with your hearts, your stories, and your prayer requests. Thank you for molding me into a strong leader and friend. You've impacted me more than you'll ever know. All of you have made my life beautiful!

About the Author

Katrina McCain is a former Fashion model from Charlotte, NC. She is the founder and president of Pearls of Hope Outreach and has a passion to encourage women of all ages to live for Jesus authentically, in spite of the culture that tells them they can't. She holds a BA in Literature and an MA in Education, from UNC-Charlotte, and is the proud wife of her husband, Jarrett, and mother to her sweet Kailyn Rhea.

To connect with Katrina or to inquire about having her speak to your women's group, please visit www.KatrinaMcCain.com

About Pearls of Hope Outreach

Pearls of Hope Outreach has been in operation since June 2013. With early beginnings as a women's small group Bible study, Pearls of Hope has now expanded into a federally recognized nonprofit organization with members all across North Carolina.

Pearls of Hope seeks to provide Godly and encouraging friendships, outreach opportunities to impact our community and positive events, which will build faith in the word of God, transform hearts to that of a servant, build genuine, loving and accountable relationships with others and ultimately compel each member to share the hope and good news of Jesus Christ in with the world: locally, nationally and globally.

For more information about Pearls of Hope Outreach, please visit www.PearlsofHopeOutreach.org

CPSIA information can be obtained
at www.ICGtesting.com
Printed in the USA
LVHW05s1902270718
585099LV00007B/36/P